Spanish Workbook for Middle School and High School Students – Grades 6-12

Vocabulary building, grammar practice for homeschool or classroom + audio to improve your pronunciation & listening skills

Illustrated by Yulia Lebedeva

Also available:

- Learn Spanish for Beginners in Audible (https://geni.us/spanishlearning)

Table of Contents

Introduction

Spanish is one of the most spoken languages around the world. No matter where you are in the world, you can find people who speak the Spanish language.

If you're an absolute beginner and learning Spanish for school, this is the best Spanish language learning resource for you! This workbook for teens has everything you need to start learning Spanish, from essential phrases and basic vocabulary to the grammar you need to help you get started creating your own sentences in Spanish. We offer:

- Essential Spanish vocabulary words and phrases
- Introduction to basic Spanish grammar
- Pronunciation guide for the Spanish alphabet
- Classroom activities to practice Spanish with your classmates
- Supplementary audio to build your Spanish listening and speaking skills (follow the Audio Download Instructions on page 135)
- Answer key
- And so much more!

This workbook was made with young adult beginners in mind. We carefully designed each lesson to be a fun and easy way to learn Spanish in school, and we hope this develops your learning habit so that you practice Spanish everyday.

We wish you the best, and good luck!

My Daily Spanish Team

El Alfabeto – The Alphabet

Let's study the alphabet in Spanish. How do the letters sound in Spanish? How do they sound in English? You can see the pronunciations below.

Listen to Track 1

Aa	ah	*ala*	alligator
Bb	beh	*bote*	boat
Cc	ceh	*centro*	center

Sometimes, the letter "C" in Spanish sounds like this: car, cotton, cocoa.

Dd	deh	*dentista*	dentist
Ee	eh	*elevador*	elevator
Ff	efeh	*fuente*	font
Gg	heh	*gente*	heritage

Similar to English, the letter "G" in Spanish can sound like the word "guess" at the beginning, but only in combination with the vowels "*a*," "*o*," and "*u*."

Gg...*ganar*   sounds like "guess"

....*gota*

....*gusano*

It will have the sound of [heh] like in "heritage" before the vowels "*e*" and "*i* ."

Gg...*gente*   sounds like "heritage"

....*girafa*

The "G" can have a strong sound, like in "guess," before "*e*" and "*i*" if you write the vowel "*u*" between them. In this case the "*u*" is not pronounced.

Gg...*guerra*   sounds like "guess"

....*guisado*

Listen to Track 2

Hh........................atcheh   *hijos*   (silent "H" in Spanish)

The letter "H" in Spanish is almost always silent. The exception is when it's a foreign word, or a word taken from another language.

Ii...............................ee	*indio*	ink
Jj..............................hota	*jarra*	jam
Kk.............................kah	*kilómetro*	kilometer
Ll..............................eleh	*lápiz*	lamb
Mm...........................emeh	*mamá*	mom
Nn.............................eneh	**n***iños*	nanny
Ñ...............................enyeh	*sue**ñ**o*	canyon
Oo.............................oh	*oso*	observe
Pp.............................peh	*perro*	pen
Qq.............................coo	*queso*	qualify
Rr..............................ereh	*reloj*	rabbit
Ss..............................eseh	*sol*	sun
Tt..............................teh	*tren*	train
Uu.............................oo	*uva*	food
Vv.............................ooveh	*verano*	vacation
Ww...................ooveh doble	windsurf	windsurf
Xx.............................eh-kis	*xilófono*	xylophone
Yy.....................ee griega	*yo-yo*	yo-yo
Zz..............................theta	*zoológico*	sound

Los Objetos del Salón de Clases – Classroom Objects

Listen to Track 3

reloj (clock)

pizarra (blackboard)

computadora (computer)

globo terráqueo (globe)

escritorio (desk)

calculadora (calculator)

cuadernos (notebooks)

silla (chair)

tijeras (scissors)

estuche de lápices (pencil case)

engrapadora (stapler)

pegamento (glue)

cinta adhesiva (scotch tape)

resaltador (highlighter)

sacapuntas (sharpener)

lápices de colores (colored pencils)

bolígrafos (pens)

borrador (eraser)

diccionario (dictionary)

crayones (crayons)

regla (ruler)

mochila (school bag)

tiza (chalk)

perforador (hole puncher)

borrador para pizarra (chalkboard eraser)

marcador (marker)

pegamento en barra (glue stick)

hoja de papel (sheet of paper)

porta papeles (clipboard)

planificador (planner)

basurero (trash can)

carpeta (folder)

materias (subjects)

Spanish speakers are especially polite when greeting. If they are sitting, they will stand to say hello or goodbye. It is common to shake hands or kiss on the cheek if the greeting is between a man and a woman.

Listen to Track 4

¡Hola!	(Hello!)
¡Buenos días!	(Good morning!)
¡Buenas tardes!	(Good afternoon!)
¡Buenas noches!	(Good evening! / Good night!)
¡Qué gusto verte!	(Nice to see you!)
¡Me alegra verte!	(I am glad to see you!)

¡Adiós!	(Good bye!)
¡Hasta luego!	(See you later!)
¡Hasta mañana!	(See you tomorrow!)
¡Nos vemos!	(See you later!)

Señor	(Mr.)
Señora	(Mrs. – Use it for older women, not for young women regardless if they are married or not.)
Señorita	(Miss or Mrs. – Use it for young women or for older women as a form of compliment.)
Joven	(There is no title for young men, so people may use the word *joven* which means "young man.")

Don	(Title of respect for a man, e.g. *don José*.)
Doña	(Title of respect for a woman, e.g. *doña María*.)

¿Qué significa...	(What does .... mean?)
Significa...	(It means...)

¡Lo siento!	(I´m sorry!)
¡Perdón!	(Sorry!)
¡Disculpe!	(Excuse me!)

Por favor	(Please)
¡Gracias!	(Thank you!)
¡De nada!	(You're welcome!)

¡Gusto en conocerte!	(Nice to meet you!)
¡El gusto es mío!	(The pleasure is mine! / My pleasure!)
¡Igualmente!	(Likewise!)

Preguntar por el Nombre – Asking about Names

To ask about someone's name, use the reflexive pronouns for each personal pronoun: **me** for *yo,* **te** for *tú,* **se** for *él, ella, usted,* and **sus** for *ellos, ellas, ustedes.*

Alternatively, you can ask for someone's name using *¿Cuál es ___ nombre?*

Listen to Track 5

¿Cómo te llamas? (tú) *¿Cuál es tu nombre?*	(What's your name?)
¿Cómo se llama? (él/ella/usted) *¿Cuál es su nombre?*	(What's his/her/ your[formal] name?)
¿Cómo se llaman (ellos/ellas/ustedes)? *¿Cuáles son sus nombres?*	(What are their/your[plural] names?)

Listen to Track 6

Practice: In groups of four, ask for each other's names in Spanish, and fill in the blanks. Don't forget to practice greeting each other in Spanish as well!

Hola, buenos días. *¿Cómo te llamas?* *Mi nombre es ______________.*	(Hello, good morning.) (What is your name?) (My name is ______________.)
¡Discúlpame, por favor! *¿Cual es su nombre?* *Su nombre es ______________.*	(Excuse me, please!) (What's his/her name?) (His/her name is ______________.)
¿Cómo se llaman? *Sus nombres son ______________.*	(What are their names?) (Their names ______________.)
¿Cuáles son sus nombres? *Nuestros nombres son ______________.*	(What are your names?) (Our names are ______________.)

Here are some ways to ask how someone is doing:

Listen to Track 7

¿Qué tal?	(How are you doing?)
¿Cómo estás?	(How are you? [informal _tú_])
¿Cómo está (él/ella/usted)?	(How is he/she?) (How are you? [formal])
¿Cómo están (ellos/ellas)?	(How are they?)

You can respond with an emotion, mood, or state of one's being.

feliz	(happy)	_confundido_	(confused)
enfadado	(angry)	_asustado_	(frightened)
deprimido	(depressed)	_cansado_	(tired)
triste	(sad)		

An adjective needs to agree with the noun's gender and number.

- For a feminine noun (females): _cansad**a**_ (tired)
- For a masculine noun (males): _cansad**o**_ (tired)
- _Feliz_ and _triste_ are exceptions, and don't modify for gender.
- To make a singular adjective plural, add an _-s_ at the end of the adjective.
- _Feliz_ is the exception: replace _-z_ with _-ces_.

Listen to Track 8

Practice: How does Susan feel today? Select an emotion from the list of adjectives given earlier in this lesson to describe how she feels.

For example: _Susan tuvo que estudiar mucho. Ella se siente cansada._
                     (Susan had to study a lot. She feels tired.)

1. _La fiesta está muy buena. Susan se siente _________________.
    (The party is very good. Susan feels _______________.)

2. *Susan vio una película de terror. Ella se siente* __________________.

   (Susan watched a horror movie. She feels ______________.)

3. *Susan se siente muy triste. Ella se siente* __________________.

   (Susan feels very sad. Susan feels ______________.)

4. *Susan no entiende ese idioma. Ella se siente* __________________.

   (Susan does not understand that language. She feels __________________.)

Answers:

1. *feliz*
2. *asustada*
3. *deprimida*
4. *confundida*

Me Gustaría Presentar… – I Would Like to Introduce…

When we want to introduce someone in a conversation, we say *"te presento a"* or *"me gustaría presentarte a"* followed by the person you want to introduce.

Listen to Track 9

Use *"te presento a,"* for informal conversation:

¡Hola, John!	(Hi, John!)
Te presento a *mi amigo Luis.*	(Let me introduce you to my friend Luis.)
¡Mucho gusto, Luis!	(It's nice to meet you, Luis!)
¡Es un placer conocerte!	(It's a pleasure!)

Listen to Track 10

Use *"me gustaría presentarte a"* for formal conversation:

¡Buenas tardes, Daniel!	(Good afternoon, Daniel!)
Me gustaría presentarte a la *Señora Ana.*	(I would like to introduce you to Mrs. Ana.)
Mucho gusto, Señora Ana.	(Nice to meet you, Mrs. Ana.)
¡El gusto es mío!	(The pleasure is mine!)

Introduce someone by their name using **a**.

Introduce someone by their title or occupation using **a el** or **a la**.

A el can be shortened to **al**. For example:

*Te presento **al** profesor de Matemáticas.*	(This is the math teacher.)

Practice: In groups of three, practice greeting and introducing one another informally. To practice informal greetings, try roleplaying as an adult, with a title such as *Señor, Señora, don,* or *doña.*

Practice: Write the conversations in English.

Listen to Track 11

Ana: *Pedro, me gustaría presentarte a mi hermano Carlos.*
Pedro: *¡Buenos días! Gusto en conocerte.*
Carlos: *El gusto es mío.*

Ana: ____
Pedro: ____
Carlos: ____

Answers:

Ana: Pedro, I would like to introduce you to my brother Carlos.
Pedro: Good morning! Nice to meet you.
Carlos: My pleasure.

Listen to Track 12

Practice: Write the conversation in Spanish.

Emily: Good afternoon Sandra. How are you?
Sandra: I feel tired. And you?

Emily: ____
Sandra: ____

Answers:

Emily: *Buenas tardes Sandra. ¿Cómo estás?*
Sandra: *Me siento cansada. ¿Y tú?*

Practice: Let's roleplay! Imagine you are someone important, with a title and name. Work in groups of three and practice introducing each other into a conversation. Decide if the situation is formal or informal and use the titles *señor*, *señora*, and *señorita* accordingly. Remember to shake hands with each other. Write one sample of your introductions on the lines below:

____

____

____

Los Números – Numbers

Here is an explanation of how to write numbers in Spanish.

Listen to Track 13

0 *cero*	7 *siete*	14 *catorce*
1 *uno*	8 *ocho*	15 *quince*
2 *dos*	9 *nueve*	16 *dieciséis*
3 *tres*	10 *diez*	17 *diecisiete*
4 *cuatro*	11 *once*	18 *dieciocho*
5 *cinco*	12 *doce*	19 *diecinueve*
6 *seis*	13 *trece*	20 *veinte*

From number 21 to number 29, you must omit the final letter *-e* from twenty, and add *-i* plus the next number.

Listen to Track 14

21 *veintiuno*	24 *veinticuatro*	27 *veintisiete*
22 *veintidós*	25 *veinticinco*	28 *veintiocho*
23 *veintitrés*	26 *veintiséis*	29 *veintinueve*

From the 30s onwards, separate the numbers and use the word *y* (and) to add another number.

Listen to Track 15

30 *treinta*	35 *treinta y cinco*
31 *treinta y uno*	36 *treinta y seis*
32 *treinta y dos*	37 *treinta y siete*
33 *treinta y tres*	38 *treinta y ocho*
34 *treinta y cuatro*	39 *treinta y nueve*

The following numbers can be written in the same way as the 30s.

Listen to Track 16

Practice writing the 40s and 50s in Spanish.

40	_cuarenta_		50	_cincuenta_
41	_______________		51	_______________
42	_______________		52	_______________
43	_______________		53	_______________
44	_______________		54	_______________
45	_______________		55	_______________
46	_______________		56	_______________
47	_______________		57	_______________
48	_______________		58	_______________
49	_______________		59	_______________

Answers:

40	_cuarenta_		50	_cincuenta_
41	_cuarenta y uno_		51	_cincuenta y uno_
42	_cuarenta y dos_		52	_cincuenta y dos_
43	_cuarenta y tres_		53	_cincuenta y tres_
44	_cuarenta y cuatro_		54	_cincuenta y cuatro_
45	_cuarenta y cinco_		55	_cincuenta y cinco_
46	_cuarenta y seis_		56	_cincuenta y seis_
47	_cuarenta y siete_		57	_cincuenta y siete_
48	_cuarenta y ocho_		58	_cincuenta y ocho_
49	_cuarenta y nueve_		59	_cincuenta y nueve_

Here are other big numbers in Spanish:

Listen to Track 17

60	*sesenta*	200	*doscientos*	700	*setecientos*
70	*setenta*	300	*trescientos*	800	*ochocientos*
80	*ochenta*	400	*cuatrocientos*	900	*novecientos*
90	*noventa*	500	*quinientos*	1,000	*mil*
100	*cien*	600	*seiscientos*	1,000,000	*un millón*

Práctica con Números – Number Practice

Listen to Track 18

Practice: Write numbers in Spanish.

319	*trescientos diecinueve*	123	
18		0	
471		45	
133		79	
59		832	
428		108	

Answers:

319	*trescientos diecinueve*	123	*ciento veintitrés*
18	*dieciocho*	0	*cero*
471	*cuatrocientos setenta y uno*	45	*cuarenta y cinco*
133	*ciento treinta y tres*	79	*setenta y nueve*
59	*cincuenta y nueve*	832	*ochocientos treinta y dos*
428	*cuatrocientos veintiocho*	108	*ciento ocho*

Listen to Track 19

Practice: Write the digital numbers for the Spanish.

seiscientos ochenta y tres		*ochocientos noventa y dos*	
doce		*cuatro*	
ochenta y uno		*quinientos veinticinco*	
doscientos dos		*setecientos trece*	
cincuenta y siete		*novecientos quince*	
trescientos veintitrés		*diecinueve*	

Answers:

seiscientos ochenta y tres	683	*ochocientos noventa y dos*	892
doce	12	*cuatro*	4
ochenta y uno	81	*quinientos veinticinco*	525
doscientos dos	202	*setecientos trece*	713
cincuenta y siete	57	*novecientos quince*	915
trescientos veintitrés	323	*diecinueve*	19

Listen to Track 20

Practice: Write the names of the numbers in the correct place:

Wordbank: *seiscientos noventa y ocho - veintitrés - trescientos ochenta dos mil trescientos veintisiete - novecientos diecinueve - cuatrocientos uno*

2,327		698	
401		380	
23		919	

Answers:

2,327	*dos mil trescientos veintisiete*	698	*seiscientos noventa y ocho*
401	*cuatrocientos uno*	380	*trescientos ochenta*
23	*veintitrés*	919	*novecientos diecinueve*

Listen to Track 21

Practice: Write the answer to the following math problems.

siete x veinticinco = _______________
trece x ocho = _______________
doscientos diez x cuatro = _______________
doce x treinta y dos = _______________

Answer:

siete x veinticinco = ciento setenta y cinco
trece x ocho = ciento cuatro
doscientos diez x cuatro = ochocientos cuarenta
doce x treinta y dos = trescientos ochenta y cuatro

Los Números Ordinales – Ordinal Numbers

Ordinal numbers are used to express the order or position of objects, people, events, and so on. Make sure that the ordinal number agrees in gender with the noun they describe. The ordinal numbers listed below are masculine. For feminine nouns, replace the *-o* ending with *-a*.

Listen to Track 22

1º *Primero* (first)	13º *Decimotercero/decimotercer* (thirteenth)
2º *Segundo* (second)	14º *Decimocuarto* (fourteenth)
3º *Tercero* (third)	15º *Decimoquinto* (fifteenth)
4º *Cuarto* (fourth)	20º *Vigésimo* (twentieth)
5º *Quinto* (fifth)	30º *Trigésimo* (thirtieth)
6º *Sexto* (sixth)	40º *Cuadragésimo* (fortieth)
7º *Séptimo* (seventh)	50º *Quincuagésimo* (fiftieth)
8º *Octavo* (eighth)	60º *Sexagésimo* (sixtieth)
9º *Noveno* (ninth)	70º *Septuagésimo* (seventieth)
10º *Décimo* (tenth)	80º *Octogésimo* (eightieth)
11º *Décimo primero/undécimo/ decimoprimer* (eleventh)	90º *Nonagésimo* (ninetieth)
12º *Decimosegundo/duodécimo* (twelfth)	100º *Centésimo* (hundredth)

Listen to Track 23

For ordinal numbers with multiple place values, add the Spanish ordinal numbers together. For example, *vigésimo* (twentieth) + *cuarto* (fourth) = *vigésimo cuarto* (twenty-fourth).

First (1st) and **third (3rd)** for **masculine nouns** drop the *-o* that is normally at the end of the ordinal number.

*Hoy es el **primer** día de clases.*	(Today is the first day of school.)
*Él es mi **tercer** hijo.*	(He is my third son.)

Listen to Track 24

Practice: Write the Spanish female and male ordinal numbers for the number below. The first problem has been done for you.

1st	primer/primero/primera	7th	______________________
10th	______________________	22nd	______________________
4th	______________________	34th	______________________

Answers:

1st primer/primero/primera	7th séptimo/séptima
10th décimo/décima	22nd vigésimo segundo/vigésima segunda
4th cuarto/cuarta	34th trigésimo cuarto/trigésima cuarta

Los Días de la Semana – The Days of the Week

It's important to know that the days of the week in Spanish are not capitalized, and are all masculine nouns.

Listen to Track 25

lunes   (Monday)

martes   (Tuesday)

miércoles   (Wednesday)

jueves   (Thursday)

viernes   (Friday)

sábado   (Saturday)

domingo   (Sunday)

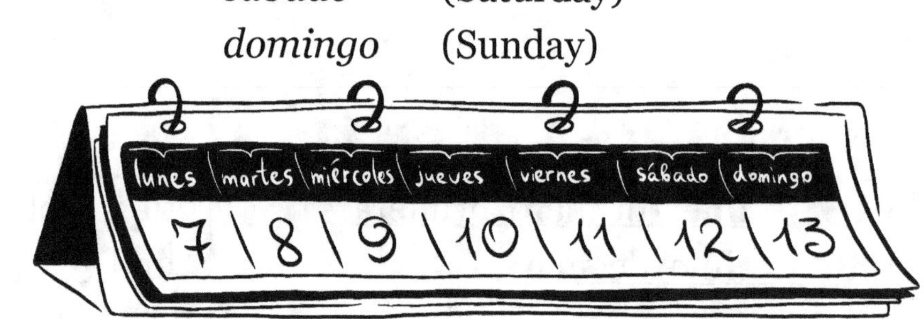

Listen to Track 26

Practice: Answer the questions by filling in the blanks, and practice talking about the days of the week in Spanish with a partner.

1. *¿Qué días te gusta ir de paseo?*
   (What days do you like to go for a walk?)

   Me gusta ir los _________________________ *y* _________________________.
   (I like to go on … and ….)

2. *¿Cuál es tu día de la semana favorito?*
   (What is your favorite day or the week?)

   Mi día de la semana favorito es el _________________________.
   (My favorite day of the week is….)

3. *¿Qué días vas a la escuela?*
   (What days do you go to school?)

   Voy a la escuela los _________________________.
   (I go to school on….)

Sample answers:

1. *Me gusta ir **los sábados** y **domingos**.*
   (I like to go on **Saturdays** and **Sundays**.)

2. *Mi día de la semana favorito es **el viernes**.*
   (My favorite day of the week is **Friday**.)

3. *Voy a la escuela **los lunes**.*
   (I go to school on **Mondays**.)

Los Meses del Año – The Months of the Year

Like the days of the week, the months in Spanish are not capitalized, and are all masculine nouns.

Listen to Track 27

enero	(January)	*julio*	(July)
febrero	(February)	*agosto*	(August)
marzo	(March)	*septiembre*	(September)
abril	(April)	*octubre*	(October)
mayo	(May)	*noviembre*	(November)
junio	(June)	*diciembre*	(December)

Listen to Track 28

Practice: Fill in the blanks with the corresponding ordinal number to complete each sentence. A few have been done for you.

1. *Enero es el ________________________ mes.*
2. *Febrero es el ________________________ mes.*
3. *Marzo es el tercero mes.*
4. *Abril es el ________________________ mes.*
5. *Mayo es el ________________________ mes.*
6. *Junio es el ________________________ mes.*
7. *Julio es el ________________________ mes.*
8. *Agosto es el octavo mes.*
9. *Septiembre es el ________________________ mes.*
10. *Octubre es el ________________________ mes.*
11. *Noviembre es el undécimo mes.*
12. *Diciembre es el ________________________ mes.*

Answers:

1. *Enero es el primer mes.*
2. *Febrero es el segundo mes.*
3. *Marzo es el tercero mes.*
4. *Abril es el cuarto mes.*
5. *Mayo es el quinto mes.*
6. *Junio es el sexto mes.*
7. *Julio es el séptimo mes.*
8. *Agosto es el octavo mes.*
9. *Septiembre es el noveno mes.*
10. *Octubre es el décimo mes.*
11. *Noviembre es el undécimo mes.*
12. *Diciembre es el duodécimo mes.*

Listen to Track 29

la estación	season
la primavera	spring
el verano	summer
el otoño	fall/autumn
el invierno	winter
la estación lluviosa	wet/rainy season (also called *el invierno*)
la estación seca	dry season (also called *el verano*)

¿Cómo es **la primavera?**	What is **spring** like?
La primavera *está llena de flores.*	(**Spring** is full of flowers.)
El verano *es muy cálido.*	(**Summer** is very warm.)
El otoño *es muy fresco.*	(**Autumn** is very cool.)
El invierno *es muy frío.*	(The **winter** is very cold.)

Listen to Track 30

Practice: Fill in the blanks and practice talking about seasons with a partner.

¿Cómo es _____________ (la estación)?	What is _____________ [season] like?
¿Cuándo es _____________ (la estación) en tu país?	(When is _____________ [season] in your country?)
En mi país, _____________ (la estación) es en _____________ (meses).	(In my country, _____________ [season] is in _____________ [month].)
Mi país no tiene _______________ (estaciones). Sólo tenemos _______________ (estaciones).	(My country does not have _______________ [seasons]. We only have _______________ [seasons].)

In Spanish, there are several ways to express weather conditions.

Listen to Track 31

En mi ciudad, hace **calor**.	(It's **hot** in my city.)
A mediodía, hace **mucho calor**.	(It's **very hot** at noon.)
En julio hace **sol**.	(It's **sunny** in July.)
La noche es **fresca** / **hace fresco**.	(The evening is **cool**.)
El verano es **soleado** *y* **caluroso**.	(Summer is **sunny** and **hot**.)
Aquí hace **frío** *en invierno*.	(It is **cold** in the winter here.)
A veces hay mucho **viento**.	(Sometimes, there is a lot of **wind**.)
Está **nublado** *ahora*.	(It's **cloudy** now.)
Hay **neblina** *en este momento*.	(There is **mist** now.)
Hace **buen tiempo** *en la primavera*.	(The **weather is nice** in the spring.)
Hay **mal tiempo**.	(There is **bad weather**.)
Está **lloviendo**.	(It's **raining**.)

Listen to Track 32

Practice: *¿Qué tiempo hace? ¿Cómo es el clima?* (How is the weather?)

With a partner, practice talking about the weather using the phrases above. You can ask questions about the weather by completing the question:

¿Cómo es el clima en...?

la mañana (the morning)	*al mediodía* (at noon)
la tarde (the afternoon)	*la noche* (at night/evening)
en tu ciudad (in your city)	*en tu país* (in your country)
en este momento/ahora (now)	*a veces* (sometimes)

Las Fechas – The Dates

The dates in Spanish are expressed as day/month/year:

Listen to Track 33

[Día] de [mes] de [año]. (The day of the month of the year.)

For example: **Hoy es 24 de junio de 2021.** (Today is June 24th, 2021.)

The first day of the month uses the ordinal number *primero*:

¿Cuándo es tu cumpleaños? (When is your birthday?)

El primero de diciembre. (The first of December.)

Regular cardinal numbers are used for subsequent dates:

El dos de diciembre. (The second of December.)

El tres de diciembre. (The third of December.)

Listen to Track 34

Practice: Write the dates in Spanish. The first one has been done for you.

December 8th	*ocho de diciembre*
July 9th	_______________________
January 14th	_______________________
April 25th	_______________________
May 15th	_______________________
February 10th	_______________________
August 1st	_______________________
November 3rd	_______________________
June 13th	_______________________

Answer key:

December 8th	*ocho de diciembre*	February 10th	*el diez de febrero*
July 9th	*el nueve de julio*	August 1st	*el primero de agosto*
January 14th	*el catorce de enero*	November 3rd	*el tres de noviembre*
April 25th	*el veinticinco de abril*	June 13th	*el trece de junio*
May 15th	*el quince de mayo*		

Subject or personal pronouns replace the name of the one performing an action within a sentence.

Listen to Track 35

yo	(I)	*vosotros*	(you - plural, masculine)
tú	(you - informal)	*vosotras*	(you - plural, feminine)
él	(he)	*nosotros*	(we - masculine)
ella	(she)	*nosotras*	(we - feminine)
usted	(you - singular, formal)	*ellos*	(they - masculine)
ustedes	(you - plural, formal)	*ellas*	(they - feminine)
vos	(you - singular, informal)		

Listen to Track 36

Practice: Substitute the subjects with the suitable personal pronouns in the following sentences. The first question has been done for you.

1. ***Julia y Carlos*** *practican deportes.* → ***Ellos*** *practican deportes.*
   (**Julia and Carlos** play sports. → **They** play sports.)

2. ***Luis*** *es muy inteligente.* → _______________________________.
   (**Luis** is very smart.)

3. ***Los estudiantes*** *leen mucho.* → _______________________________.
   (**The students** read a lot.)

4. ***Beatriz*** *trabaja mucho.* → _______________________________.
   (**Beatriz** works a lot.)

5. ***Mis padres*** *comen pescado.* → _______________________________.
   (**My parents** eat fish.)

Answers:

2. ***Luis*** *es muy inteligente.* → ***Él*** *es muy inteligente.*
3. ***Los estudiantes*** *leen mucho.* → ***Ellos*** *leen mucho.*
4. ***Beatriz*** *trabaja mucho.* → ***Ella*** *trabaja mucho.*
5. ***Mis padres*** *comen pescado.* → ***Ellos*** *comen pescado.*

Los Sustantivos y sus Géneros – Nouns and their Genders

Listen to Track 37

Masculine nouns almost always end with an *-o*, *-e*, *-r*, or *-s*.

Masculine nouns ending in *-o*	Masculine nouns ending in *-e*
perro (dog)	*puente* (bridge)
niño (boy)	*viaje* (trip)
cerebro (brain)	*cine* (movie theater)

Masculine nouns ending in *-r*	Masculine nouns ending in *-s*
amanecer (dawn)	*compás* (compass)
atardecer (sunset)	*lunes* (Monday)
anochecer (dusk/nightfall)	*cumpleaños* (birthday)

Listen to Track 38

Feminine nouns often end with *-a* or *-ión*.

Feminine nouns ending with *-a*	Feminine nouns ending *-ión*
magia (magic)	*canción* (song)
casa (house/home)	*religión* (religion)
mamá (mother)	

It's important to note that these are not fixed rules; there are exceptions.

Listen to Track 39

Masculine exceptions	Feminine exceptions
el día (day)	*la foto* (photo)
el problema (problem)	*la tarde* (afternoon)

Practice: Search for nouns in this workbook, and add them to the list in this section.
Note the genders, and exceptions.

Sustantivos en Plural – Plural Nouns

There are basic rules to follow when making a singular noun plural.

Listen to Track 40

Nouns ending in a vowel : add -*s*

casa	→	casa**s**
ave	→	ave**s**
hermano	→	hermano**s**

Nouns ending in a consonant : add -*es*

| canción | → | cancion**es** |
| televisor | → | televisor**es** |

Nouns ending in -s : no change

cumpleaños

oasis

lunes

Nouns ending in -z : replace -z with -*ces*

| audaz | → | auda**ces** |
| aprendiz | → | aprendi**ces** |

Listen to Track 41

Practice: Write the plural forms of the following nouns.

1. *libro* _____________________
2. *animal* _____________________
3. *teléfono* _____________________
4. *ensalada* _____________________
5. *maleta* _____________________
6. *arroz* _____________________

Answers:

1. *libros*
2. *animales*
3. *teléfonos*
4. *ensaladas*
5. *maletas*
6. *arroces*

Los Artículos – Articles

Articles go before a noun and show whether it is definite or indefinite.

Listen to Track 42

Artículos definidos (definite articles, like "the" in English)

Definite articles are used to express that the noun is specific. For example, "the blue pencil" refers to one particular blue pencil.

la   "the" feminine, singular.
las   "the" feminine, plural.
el   "the" masculine, singular.
los   "the" masculine (or masculine and feminine), plural.

Listen to Track 43

Practice: Fill in the spaces with the corresponding definite articles:

1. _________ *barco es muy grande.* (The boat is very big.)
2. _________ *casa es bonita.* (The house is beautiful.)
3. _________ *camisas están limpias.* (The shirts are clean.)
4. _________ *estudiantes son felices.* (The students are happy.)

Answer key:

1. *El barco es muy grande.*
2. *La casa es bonita.*
3. *Las camisas están limpias.*
4. *Los estudiantes son felices.*

Listen to Track 44

Artículos indefinidos (indefinite articles, like "a/an" or "some" in English)

Used for a noun that is not specific. For example, "a blue pencil" could be any blue pencil, not one blue pencil in particular.

un "a/an" Masculine, singular.
una "a/an" Feminine, singular.
unos "some/a few" Masculine (or masculine and feminine), plural.
unas "some/a few" Feminine, plural.

Listen to Track 45

Practice: Fill in the spaces with the corresponding indefinite article.

1. *Rodrigo tiene ___________ sueño.*
   (Rodrigo has a dream.)
2. *Los estudiantes compraron _____________ libros interesantes.*
   (The students bought some interesting books.)
3. *A mi papá le gustaría tener _____________ mascota.*
   (My father would like to have a pet.)

Answers:

1. *Rodrigo tiene <u>un</u> sueño.*
   (Rodrigo has a dream.)
2. *Los estudiantes compraron <u>unos</u> libros interesantes.*
   (The students bought some interesting books.)
3. *A mi papá le gustaría tener <u>una</u> mascota.*
   (My father would like to have a pet.)

In Spanish the expression *¿qué es?* is used for singular nouns, and *¿qué son?* to talk about plural nouns.

Listen to Track 46

¿Qué es?	(What is it?)
¿Qué son?	(What are they/those?)
Es un/una... (indefinite article)	(It is a/an...)
Es el/la... (definite article)	(It is the...)

Practice: Point at random things you can find, and ask *¿Qué es?* or *¿Qué son?*

Sample answers:

Listen to Track 47

¿Qué es?	What is it?
Es el libro que quieres.	It is the book that you want.
¿Qué son?	What are they?
Son las frutas que compré.	They are the fruits that I bought.

The questions *¿Qué es?* and *¿Qué son?* in Spanish are commonly used with the demonstratives to complete the expression, or supplement the question with more information.

Listen to Track 48

esto / esta (this)	*estos / estas* (these)
eso / aquello (that)	*esos / aquellos* (those)

¿Qué es esto / esta?	(What is this?)
¿Qué es eso / aquello?	(What is that?)
¿Qué son estos / estas?	(What are these?)
¿Qué son esos /aquellos (+ nouns)?	(What are those [+ nouns]?)

Los Adjetivos – Adjectives

Adjectives in Spanish must match the noun they describe in gender and number. Let's cover the basic rules for gender and number agreements for adjectives.

Listen to Track 49

Adjectives ending with -o are for masculine nouns. For feminine nouns, replace the -o with an **-a**.

> _Él está content**o**. → Ella está content**a**._

Adjectives ending with -e or a consonant _usually_ have no gender agreements. In other words, the word won't change whether it modifies a feminine noun or a masculine noun.

> _Él es interesante. → Ella es interesante._

The exceptions for adjectives ending with a consonant are if they describe someone's **nationality**, or end with **-án, -ín, -ón**, or **-or**. For these exceptions, add an **-a** at the end.

> _el hombre español_ → la mujer español**a**
> _el doctor_ → la doctor**a**

Now let's talk about plural adjectives.

Listen to Track 50

Adjectives ending with a vowel just need to add an **-s** to the end.

> _la niña linda_ → _las niñas linda**s**_
> _el gato pequeño_ → _los gatos pequeño**s**_

Adjectives ending with a consonant just need to add **-es** to the end to make it plural.

> _fácil_ → _fácil**es**_
> _especial_ → _especial**es**_

Adjectives ending with -z become plural by replacing -z with **-ces**.

> _el niño feliz_ → _los niños feli**ces**_
> _Él es capaz. → Todos son capa**ces**._

When describing a group of nouns, even if the group of nouns have both genders, we always use the **masculine** form. In other words, we'd use the article *los* and the subject pronouns *nosotros*, *vosotros*, and *ellos*.

la niña + el niño = los niños
mi hermana + mi hermano + yo = nosotros
él + ella = ellos
mamá + papá = los padres

Listen to Track 51

Practice: Complete the sentences with the adjective. Make sure that the adjectives agree with the nouns that they modify.

bonito (beautiful)   *caro* (expensive)   *lindo* (cute)
grande (big)   *pequeño* (small)

1. *Carolina es* ___________________. (Caroline is small.)
2. *La noche está* ___________________. (The night is beautiful.)
3. *El anillo es muy* ___________________. (The ring is very expensive.)
4. *Los aviones son* ___________________. (The airplanes are big.)
5. *Mis hermanas son* ___________________. (My sisters are cute.)

Answers:

1. *Carolina es <u>pequeña</u>.* (Caroline is small.)
2. *La noche está <u>bonita</u>.* (The night is beautiful.)
3. *El anillo es muy <u>caro</u>.* (The ring is very expensive.)
4. *Los aviones son <u>grandes</u>.* (The airplanes are big.)
5. *Mis hermanas son <u>lindas</u>.* (My sisters are cute.)

Like in the examples above, adjectives are usually placed **after** the noun they describe in Spanish.

However, there are some instances when adjectives are placed before a noun. This is usually done to emphasize the adjective, or to describe a noun's quantity or numbers. For example:

Listen to Track 52

¡Qué <u>bonita</u> tarde! (What a beautiful evening!)
Es una <u>excelente</u> experiencia. (It is an excellent experience.)
Ellas tienen <u>dos</u> carros. (They have two cars.)
Hay <u>mucha</u> gente. (There are a lot of people.)

Listen to Track 53

Practice: Highlight the option that has the best adjective order.

1. *Yo leo muchos libros/libros muchos.* (I read a lot of books.)
2. *Nosotros somos amigos buenos/buenos amigos.* (We are good friends.)
3. *Tienes veinte bolígrafos/bolígrafos veinte.* (You have twenty pens.)
4. *¿Cuáles son tus favoritas canciones/canciones favoritas?*
   (What are your favorite songs?)
5. *Mi mamá es una mujer tímida/tímida mujer.* (My mom is a shy woman.)

Answers:

1. *muchos libros*
2. *buenos amigos*
3. *veinte bolígrafos*
4. *canciones favoritas*
5. *mujer tímida*

Los Colores – Colors

Colors are adjectives that can be located before or after the noun they describe.

Listen to Track 54

rojo (red)   *azul* (blue)   *negro* (black)
anaranjado (orange)   *morado* (purple)   *blanco* (white)
amarillo (yellow)   *rosado* (pink)
verde (green)   *café/marrón* (brown)

Colors that go after a noun must agree with the noun's gender and number. If the noun is female, replace the *-o* ending with *-a*. If the noun is plural, add an *-s* at the end of the color.

Listen to Track 55

For example: *un<u>as</u> computador<u>as</u> blanc<u>as</u>* (some white computers)

The exceptions are the colors *marrón* (brown), *café* (brown), and *verde* (green). They have no gender agreements, but become *marrones, cafés,* and *verdes* respectively after a plural noun.

When asking about the color of something, you say:

¿De qué color es... ?   What color is... ? (singular)

¿De qué color son... ?   What color are... ? (plural)

Practice: In pairs, think about the following objects and ask your classmate what color each item is:

Listen to Track 56

la casa (house)
las flores (flowers)
la mesa (table)
los libros (books)
el abrigo (coat)

el gato (cat)
el cielo (sky)
las manzanas (apples)
los mangos (mangoes)

Listen to Track 57

Sample answers:

¿De qué color es su abrigo?
(What color is your coat?)

Es rojo.
(It's red.)

¿De qué color son las flores?
(What color are the flowers?)

Son blancas.
(They're white.)

La Posesión – Possession

We use possessive adjectives to express ownership or possession of an object.

Listen to Track 58

mi (my)   *nuestro/nuestra* (our)
tu (your)   *vuestro/vuestra* (your)
su (his, her, its, their, your [formal or plural])

For plural nouns or multiple objects, add an *-s* to the possessive adjective.

Listen to Track 59

Practice: Complete the translation of these phrases in Spanish.

1. My school   ___________________ *escuela*
2. Your apartment   ___________________ *apartamento*
3. His fruits   ___________________ *frutas*
4. Our (masculine) last names   ___________________ *apellidos*
5. Our (feminine) house   ___________________ *casa*
6. Your (plural) name   ___________________ *nombre*

Answers:

1. *Mi escuela*
2. *Tu apartamento*
3. *Sus frutas*
4. *Nuestros apellidos*
5. *Nuestra casa*
6. *Vuestro nombre*

Another way to express possession in Spanish is by using **de** in this formula:

[object] + **de** + **[subject]**

Listen to Track 60

De is used before a name. **De la** or **de el** go before a title or profession, like *Señor* or or *el doctor*. Note: **de** + **el** = **del**.

*Estamos en el restaurante **del** papá **de** Mary.* (We are in Mary**'s** dad**'s** restaurant.)

Listen to Track 61

Practice: Fill in the blanks with either *de* or *del* possessives.

1. *¿Qué hay en la cocina_____________ Mary?* (What is there in Mary's kitchen?)
2. *¡Trae la maleta _____________ abuelo!* (Bring grandpa's suitcase!)
3. *Este libro es _____________ amigo de Juan.* (This book belongs to Juan's friend.)
4. *¡Vamos a la tienda _____________ Carlos!* (Let's go to Carlos' store!)

Answers:

1. *¿Qué hay en la cocina <u>de</u> Mary?*
2. *¡Trae la maleta <u>del</u> abuelo!*
3. *Este libro es <u>del</u> amigo de Juan.*
4. *¡Vamos a la tienda <u>de</u> Carlos!*

Activity: ¿Conoces a mi Familia? – Do you Know my Family?

Listen to Track 62

Mi familia es grande.	My family is big.
Daniel es mi papá. Es ingeniero.	Daniel is my father. He is an engineer.
Mi mamá se llama Carla. Le gusta mucho cocinar.	My mother's name is Carla. She likes to cook.
Tengo una hermana. Su nombre es Ana y tiene cinco años.	I have a sister. Her name is Ana and she is five years old.
Tengo dos hermanos varones, con quienes estudio en la escuela.	I have two brothers, with whom I study at school.
Sus nombres son Andrés y Carlos (lo llamamos Carlitos).	Their names are Andrés and Carlos (we call him Carlitos).
Mis abuelos paternos viven en Francia.	My paternal grandparents live in France.
Mi abuela se llama Lucía.	My grandmother's name is Lucia.
Mi abuelo se llama David.	My grandfather's name is David.
Mis abuelos maternos viven en Canadá.	My maternal grandparents live in Canada.
Mi tío es gracioso. Mi tía siempre se ríe. Viven en Australia.	My uncle is funny. My aunt is always laughing. They live in Australia.
A mis primos les gusta leer.	My cousins like to read.
Estoy muy feliz de tener a mi familia.	I am very happy to have my family.

Listen to Track 63

Practice: Describe your family. Try making your own descriptions based on the sentences given above. Use the possessive *mi* (my) when possible.

Sample answers:

Mi familia no es grande. José es mi papá. Es profesor. Mi mamá se llama Mary. Le gusta mucho trabajar.

"Hay..." – There Is... / There Are...

What do you see in this city?

The Spanish word to express existence is *hay.* In many cases, it is followed by an indefinite article or other words that express amounts. But in other cases, it is followed by different types of words.

Listen to Track 64

*En mi ciudad **hay** muchos árboles.*	There are many trees in my city.
***Hay** también una torre muy grande.*	There is also a big tower.
*No **hay** un tren.*	There is no train.
***Hay** muchos buses.*	There are many buses.
*También **hay** un aeropuerto.*	There is also an airport.

Listen to Track 65

Practice:

In pairs, ask and answer questions about what is in your city.

¿Qué hay en tu ciudad?	What is there in your city?
En mi ciudad hay _____________.	There is_____________ in my city.
¿Hay _________ en tu ciudad?	Is there _______ in your city?

Sample answers:

En mi ciudad hay un tren.	There is a train in my city.
¿Hay muchos taxis en tu ciudad?	Are there many taxis in your city?
Sí, en mi ciudad hay muchos taxis.	Yes, there are many taxis in my city.
En mi ciudad hay mucha gente.	There are many people in my city.
En mi ciudad hay un centro comercial.	There is a shopping center in my city.

Los Verbos – Verbs

Verbs in their basic form are called infinitive verbs. In English, the infinitive verb has "to" before it, but in Spanish, infinitive verbs have a verb stem and an ending that needs to be changed in different circumstances.

English infinitive verbs: **to** like, **to** speak, **to** do, etc.

Listen to Track 66

Spanish infinitive verbs: *gustar, correr, subir*, etc.

As you can see above, Spanish verbs have infinitive forms ending in *-ar*, *-er*, and *-ir*. Those endings will change depending on what the verb is being used for; this is called conjugation. Here's how you conjugate or change a Spanish verb:

- First, take a verb in infinitive form, such as *gustar*.
- Identify the root (*gust-*) from the ending (*-ar*).
- Replace the ending (*-ar*) with the conjugated ending, according to subject and tense.

Once you become familiar with basic conjugation rules, you'll be comfortable with using verbs in different tenses in no time!

Listen to Track 67

Practice: Separate the following verbs' roots from their endings:

For example: *gustar* (to like): *gust-* + *-ar*

1. *abrir* (to open): _______________________
2. *aprender* (to learn): _______________________
3. *cantar* (to sing): _______________________
4. *correr* (to run): _______________________
5. *escribir* (to write): _______________________
6. *describir* (to describe): _______________________

Answers:

1. *abrir* (to open): *abr-* + *-ir*
2. *aprender* (to learn): *aprend-* + *-er*
3. *cantar* (to sing): *cant-* + *-ar*
4. *correr* (to run): *corr-* + *-er*
5. *escribir* (to write): *escrib-* + *-ir*
6. *describir* (to describe): *describ-* + *-ir*

Verbos Que Terminan En "-Ar" – Verbs Ending In "-Ar"

All regular verbs that finish with *-ar* have the same ending when conjugated. Follow these simple rules with them:

1. Find the infinitive form of a verb ending with *-ar*.
2. Replace the *-ar* ending with the conjugation according to the subject and tense.

These are the endings for each subject in the simple present tense:

Listen to Track 68

Subject	Ending	Example - *cantar* (to sing)
Yo	-o	canto
Tú	-as	cantas
Vos	-ás	cantás
Él, ella, usted	-a	canta
Nosotros, nosotras	-amos	cantamos
Vosotros, vosotras	-áis	cantáis
Ustedes	-an	cantan
Ellos, ellas	-an	cantan

Practice: Write the correct conjugation of the following regular verbs:

Subject	*hablar* (to talk)	*comprar* (to buy)	*respirar* (to breathe)	*nadar* (to swim)
Yo				
Tú				
Él, ella, usted				
Vos				
Nosotros/as				
Vosotros/as				
Ustedes				
Ellos, ellas				

Listen to Track 69

Answers:

Subject	*hablar* (to talk)	*comprar* (to buy)	*respirar* (to breathe)	*nadar* (to swim)
Yo	*hablo*	*compro*	*respiro*	*nado*
Tú	*hablas*	*compras*	*respiras*	*nadas*
Él, ella , usted	*habla*	*compra*	*respira*	*nada*
Vos	*hablás*	*comprás*	*respirás*	*nadás*
Nosotros/as	*hablamos*	*compramos*	*respiramos*	*nadamos*
Vosotros/as	*habláis*	*compráis*	*respiráis*	*nadáis*
Ustedes	*hablan*	*compran*	*respiran*	*nadan*
Ellos, ellas	*hablan*	*compran*	*respiran*	*nadan*

Here are some other useful regular *-ar* verbs:

Listen to Track 70

saltar (to jump)	*viajar* (to travel)	*estudiar* (to study)	*preguntar* (to ask)
pintar (to paint)	*trabajar* (to work)	*llorar* (to cry)	*terminar* (to finish)

Write the following sentences in Spanish:

English	Spanish
They study.	*Ellos*
She asks.	
You travel.	*Tú*
I work.	
We finish.	*Nosotros*
He paints.	
You cry.	*Ustedes*
You jump.	*Vos*

Listen to Track 71

Answers:

English	Spanish
They study.	*Ellos estudian.*
She asks.	*Ella pregunta.*
You travel.	*Tú viajas.*
I work.	*Yo trabajo.*
We finish.	*Nosotros terminamos.*
He paints.	*Él pinta.*
You cry.	*Ustedes lloran.*
You jump.	*Vos saltás.*

"Estar" – To Be

Subject	*estar* (to be)
Yo	*estoy*
Tú	*estás*
Él, ella, usted	*está*
Vos	*estás*
Vosotros, vosotras	*estáis*
Nosotros, nosotras	*estamos*
Ustedes	*están*
Ellos, ellas	*están*

The verb *estar* is not a regular *-ar* verb; it's irregular. Its use is to convey a mood, temporary condition, location, or temporary activity (combined with another verb in *-iendo* or *-ando* form.)

How to express **mood** with the verb *estar*:

Listen to Track 73

Carlos está triste.	(Carlos is sad.)
Los niños están felices.	(The kids are happy.)
Susan está contenta.	(Susan is glad.)

How to express a **temporary condition** with the verb *estar*:

Listen to Track 74

Luis está listo para su foto.	(Luis is ready for his photo.)
La mesa está un poco sucia.	(The table is a little dirty.)

How to talk about **location** with *estar*:

Listen to Track 75

La familia está en el parque.	(The family is in the park.)
Mi profesor está en la escuela.	(My teacher is at school.)
Luis está en la oficina.	(Luis is at the office.)

How to express **temporary activity** with *estar*:

In these cases, estar acts as an auxiliary verb, and it's necessary to give the second verb the ending *-iendo* or *-ando*. This is a lot like the English "-ing."

Listen to Track 76

*Víctor **está** estudi**ando**.*   (Victor is studying.)
*Carla **está** corr**iendo**.*   (Carla is running.)
*Benjamín **está** trabaj**ando**.*   (Benjamin is working.)

Listen to Track 77

Practice: Fill in the blanks with *estar*. Write in the parentheses the idea it expresses, whether it's a mood, temporary condition, location, or temporary activity.

1. *Carolina ___________ feliz por sus buenas notas.* (   )
   (Carolina is happy about her grades.)

2. *Carlos ___________ preparado para salir.* (   )
   (Carlos is ready to leave.)

3. *Beatriz ___________ en el parque con su familia.* (   )
   (Beatriz is in the park with her family.)

4. *Mis amigas ___________ disfrutando en la playa.* (   )
   (My friends are enjoying themselves at the beach.)

5. *No ___________ cocinando la cena.* (   )
   (We are not cooking dinner.)

6. *¿ ___________ enojado?* (   )
   (Are you angry?)

Answers:

1. *Carolina <u>está</u> feliz por sus buenas notas.* (mood)
   (Carolina is happy about her grades.)

2. *Carlos <u>está</u> preparado para salir.* (temporary condition)
   (Carlos is ready to leave.)

3. *Beatriz <u>está</u> en el parque con su familia.* (location)
   (Beatriz is in the park with her family.)

4. *Mis amigas <u>están</u> disfrutando en la playa.* (temporary activity)
   (My friends are enjoying themselves at the beach.)

5. *No <u>estamos</u> cocinando la cena.* (temporary activity)
   (We are not cooking dinner.)

6. *¿<u>Estás</u> enojado?* (mood)
   (Are you angry?)

Las Partes de Una Casa – The Parts of a House

To express existence in Spanish, the expression *hay* (there is) is used.

Practice: What objects belong in each room of the house? Sort the objects below to the room they belong to.

Listen to Track 78

la mesa de centro (coffee table)
las flores (flowers)
el refrigerador (refrigerator)
las plantas (plants)
la mesa de comedor (dining table)
el sofá (sofa)
las herramientas (tools)
el armario (closet)

la ducha/regadera (shower)
la televisión (television)
el lavamanos (sink)
la bañera (bathtub)
el fregadero (kitchen sink)
la cama (bed)
el horno (oven)
las sillas (chairs)

En la sala (living room), *hay*	*En la cocina* (kitchen), *hay*
En el comedor (dining room), *hay*	*En la habitación* (bedroom), *hay*
En el baño (bathroom), *hay*	*En el jardín* (garden/yard), *hay*

Answers:

Listen to Track 79

En la sala (living room), _hay_
  • _el sofá_ (sofa)
  • _la televisión_ (television)
  • _la mesa de centro_ (coffee table)
	En la cocina (kitchen), _hay_
	  • _el fregadero (kitchen sink)_
	  • _el horno (oven)_
	  • _el refrigerador_ (refrigerator)

En el comedor (dining room), _hay_
  • _la mesa de comedor_ (dining table)
  • _las sillas_ (chairs)
	En la habitación (bedroom), _hay_
	  • _el armario_ (closet)
	  • _la cama_ (bed)

En el baño (bathroom), _hay_
  • _la bañera_ (bathtub)
  • _el lavamanos_ (sink)
  • _la ducha/regadera_ (shower)
	En el jardín (garden/yard), _hay_
	  • _las herramientas_ (tools)
	  • _las flores_ (flowers)
	  • _las plantas_ (plants)

Use the verb *estar* to ask and answer questions about the location of objects or people. If the object is singular, use *está*. If it is plural, use *están*.

Listen to Track 80

Practice: Answer the questions in Spanish.

Example: *¿Dónde está la computadora? (en la mesa)*
        Está en la mesa.

        Where is the computer? (on the table)
        It's on the table.

¿Dónde está mi lápiz? (en la mochila) _______________________
(Where is my pencil? [in the backpack])

¿Dónde está mi papá? (en la sala) _______________________
(Where is my father? [in the living room])

¿Dónde están los libros? (en el librero) _______________________
(Where are the books? [in the library])

¿Dónde está mi cama? (en tu cuarto) _______________________
(Where is my bed? [in your room])

¿Dónde está el perro? (en el patio) _______________________
(Where is the dog? [in the yard])

¿Dónde está mi plato? (en la cocina) _______________________
(Where is my plate? [in the kitchen])

¿Dónde está el carro? (en el taller mecánico) _______________________
(Where is the car? [in the garage])

¿Dónde están las tijeras? (en el estuche) _______________________
(Where are the scissors? [in the pencil case])

¿Dónde está mi cepillo? (en el baño) _______________________
(Where is my brush? [in the bathroom])

¿Dónde están mis botas? (en el piso) _______________________
(Where are my boots? [on the floor])

¿Dónde están mis calcetines? (en el canasto) _______________________
(Where are my socks? [in the basket])

Answers:

¿Dónde está mi lápiz? — *Está en la mochila.*
¿Dónde está mi papá? — *Está en la sala.*
¿Dónde están los libros? — *Están en el librero.*
¿Dónde está mi cama? — *Está en tu cuarto.*
¿Dónde está el perro? — *Está en el patio.*
¿Dónde está mi plato? — *Está en la cocina.*
¿Dónde está el carro? — *Está en el taller mecánico.*
¿Dónde están las tijeras? — *Están en el estuche.*
¿Dónde está mi cepillo? — *Está en el baño.*
¿Dónde están mis botas? — *Están en el piso.*
¿Dónde están mis calcetines? — *Están en el canasto.*

Las Preposiciones – Prepositions

In the Spanish language, the classifications of prepositions are extensive. Please note that this chapter will only introduce you to common prepositions.

Listen to Track 81

con (with)	*Sheyla está **con** su mamá.* (Sheyla is **with** her mother.)
de (of)	*Esta es una foto **de** mi familia.* (This is a picture **of** my family.)
de (from [place])	*Julia es **de** Inglaterra.* (Julia is **from** England.)
desde (from [time])	*Yo estudio **desde** las 7:00 am.* (I study **from** 7:00 am.)
en (in [place])	*Carlos vive **en** Europa.* (Carlos lives **in** Europe.)
en (on [place])	*Mi lápiz está **en** el escritorio.* (My pencil is **on** the desk.)
en (in [time])	*El cumpleaños de mi prima es **en** mayo.* (My cousin's birthday is **in** May.)
entre (between)	*El florero está **entre** la mesa y el radio.* (The vase is **between** the table and the radio.)
hacia (towards)	*El gato camina **hacia** la puerta.* (The cat walks **towards** the door.)
para (for)	*Este regalo es **para** mi maestra.* (This present is **for** my teacher.)
sin (without)	*¡No tomes mis cosas **sin** preguntar!* (Don't take my stuff **without** asking!)
sobre (on)	*Mi cuaderno está **sobre** la mesa.* (My notebook is **on** the table.)

Listen to Track 82

Practice: Fill in the blanks with the correct preposition.

1. *Sofía, ¿sabes dónde está mi sacapuntas?*
   (Sofia, do you know where my sharpener is?)

   Sí, está ___________ el escritorio.
   (Yes, it's **on** the desk.)

2. *Tengo que ir ___________ la entrada principal del teatro.*
   (I have to go **towards** the main entrance of the theater.)

3. *Siempre compro un regalo ___________ mi mamá.*
   (I always buy a gift **for** my mom.)

4. *Mis amigos van al cine ___________ sus padres.*
   (My friends go to the movies **with** their parents.)

5. *Hay un jardín delante ___________ la casa.*
   (There is a garden in front **of** the house.)

6. *Sofía sale de casa ___________ su paraguas.*
   (Sofia leaves the house **without** her umbrella.)

7. *¿___________ dónde eres?*
   (Where are you **from**?)

8. *Estoy ___________ el centro comercial.*
   (I'm **in** the shopping mall.)

Answers:

1. *sobre*
2. *hacia*
3. *para*
4. *con*
5. *de*
6. *sin*
7. *De*
8. *en*

El Gerundio – The Gerund

In Spanish, we can say "is ____-ing" by conjugating *estar* with a gerund. To form the gerund, verbs ending in *-ar* change their ending to *-ando,* and verbs ending in *-er* or *-ir* change the ending to *-iendo.*

Listen to Track 83

estudiar (to study)   *estar + estudiando* (to be + studying)

David está estudiando. (David is studying.)

aprender (to learn)   *estar + aprendiendo* (to be + learning)

Susan está aprendiendo español. (Susan is learning Spanish.)

abrir (to open)   *estar + abriendo* (to be + opening)

Daniel está abriendo su regalo. (Daniel is opening his gift.)

Listen to Track 84

Practice: Write the gerund form of each verb.

caminar (to walk)		romper (to break)	
hablar (to speak)		tener (to have)	
usar (to use)		abrir (to open)	
viajar (to travel)		decidir (to decide)	
beber (to drink)		escribir (to write)	
comer (to eat)		vivir (to live)	

Answer key:

caminar (to walk)	caminando	romper (to break)	rompiendo
hablar (to speak)	hablando	tener (to have)	teniendo
usar (to use)	usando	abrir (to open)	abriendo
viajar (to travel)	viajando	decidir (to decide)	decidiendo
beber (to drink)	bebiendo	escribir (to write)	escribiendo
comer (to eat)	comiendo	vivir (to live)	viviendo

¿Qué Haces? – What are You Doing?

When asked *¿qué haces?* (what are you doing?), you need to reply with the present progressive:

Listen to Track 85

Subject + *estar* **(conjugated) + gerund (verb ending with** *-iendo* **or** *-ando***).**

Here are some possible answers to the question *¿qué haces?*

Estoy estudiando.	(I am studying.)
Mi familia está comiendo en el parque.	(My family is eating in the park.)
Caroline está comiendo sopa.	(Caroline is eating soup.)

Practice: Today is Benjamin's birthday. Match the Spanish to the English.

Listen to Track 86

1: *Los amigos de Benjamín están comiendo en la fiesta.*	A: The children are celebrating Benjamin's birthday.
2: *Benjamín está soplando las velas de la torta.** **Torta* means "cake." Depending on the country, there are many ways to say "cake" in Spanish, like *pastel* and *tarta.*	B: Benjamin's mother is buying many gifts for him.
3: *Los niños están celebrando el cumpleaños de Benjamín.*	C: Benjamin is blowing out the candles on the cake.
4: *La mamá de Benjamín está comprando muchos regalos para él.*	D: Benjamin's friends are eating at the party.

Answer key:

1. D
2. C
3. A
4. B

"Ser" – To Be

Subject	*ser* (to be)
Yo	*soy*
Tú	*eres*
Él, ella, usted	*es*
Vos	*sos*
Vosotros, vosotras	*sois*
Nosotros, nosotras	*somos*
Ustedes	*son*
Ellos, ellas	*son*

The verb *ser* (to be) is an irregular verb that describes a subject's basic traits that cannot be easily changed. Let's talk about how to use *ser* to describe one's nature.

A. To describe personality traits and relationships. It can also describe personal characteristics such as physical appearance and age.

Example: **Soy** *inteligente.* (I am intelligent.)
Eres *mi amigo.* (You are my friend.)
Mi abuela **es** *vieja.* (My grandmother is old.)
Ellos **son** *altos.* (They are tall.)

B. To talk about occupations.

Example: *Sheyla* **es** *enfermera.* (Sheyla is a nurse.)
Carlos **es** *un profesor.* (Carlos is a teacher.)

C. To describe someone's *gentilicio* or nationality.

Example: *Mis amigos* **son** *colombianos.* (My friends are Colombian.)
Lucía **es** *de España.* (Lucía is from Spain.)

D. To describe one's religion:

Example: *Mi tío* **es** *sacerdote.* (My uncle is a priest.)
Daniela **es** *una cristiana verdadera.* (Daniela is a true Christian.)

Listen to Track 89

Practice: Fill in the blank with a conjugated form of *ser* in present tense.

1. *Alex* __________ *un ingeniero.* (Alex **is** an engineer.)
2. *Nosotros* __________ *de Japón.* (We **are** from Japan.)
3. *¿* __________ *una pianista?* (**Are** you a pianist?)
4. *Mis amigos* __________ *escritores.* (My friends **are** writers.)
5. *Daniel* __________ *un excelente papá.* (Daniel **is** an excellent father.)
6. __________ *extranjeros.* (They **are** foreigners.)
7. __________ *estudiante.* (**I'm** a student.)

Answers:

1. *es*
2. *somos*
3. *Eres*
4. *son*
5. *es*
6. *Son*
7. *Soy*

Practice: Write about yourself using *ser*. Use the examples in this section to help you describe yourself. Then with a partner, take turns talking about yourselves.

____

____

____

____

____

____

Otros Usos De "Ser" – Other Uses of "To Be"

The verb *ser* (to be) is also used to describe objects according to their number, color, shape, and size. Don't forget that verbs must agree in gender and number with the noun they are describing!

Listen to Track 90

La casa **es** *grande.*	The house is big.
Esas flores **son** *pequeñas y amarillas.*	Those flowers are small and yellow.
Somos *tres en mi familia.*	We are three (There are three of us) in my family.

We can also use the verb *ser* to tell the time:

Listen to Track 91

¿Qué hora **es?**	(What time is it?)
Son las _____ *am/pm.*	(It's _________ am/pm.)

We use *"es"* to **ask** for the time, and *"son las"* to **tell** the time. The only exception is if it is 1:00 pm.

¿Qué hora **es?**	(What time is it?)
Es la *1:00 pm.*	(It is 1:00 pm.)

Use the verb *ser* to tell the date:

Listen to Track 92

Hoy **es** *25 de noviembre.*	(Today is November 25th.)
Mi cumpleaños **es** *el 12 de abril.*	(My birthday is on April 12th.)

When talking about possessions:

Listen to Track 93

¿Ese diccionario **es** *tuyo?*	(Is that dictionary yours?)
Esos **son** *mis zapatos.*	(Those are my shoes.)

"Ser" Vs. "Estar" – To Be

Ser and *estar* are both verbs meaning "to be" in English. But how can you tell the difference?

Estar is used to describe a **temporary characteristic** or disposition, such as mood, activity, or location at a certain point in time.

Ser is used to describe **permanent characteristics,** such as physical traits, occupation, faith, and personality, which are not likely to change anytime soon. *Ser* is also used to talk about the date and time, descriptions, and possessions.

Read the following conversation. Choose one color to highlight the verb **ser** and a different color to highlight the verb **estar.**

Listen to Track 94

Alberto: Hola, Javier ¿Cómo estás? (Hi, Javier, how are you?)

Javier: Muy bien, ¿y tú?, Alberto. (Very well, and you, Alberto?)

Alberto: Bien, gracias. Te presento a mi amiga Ana. (Well, thank you. This is my friend Ana.)

Javier: Mucho gusto, Ana ¿Eres la hermana de Juan? (Nice to meet you, Ana. Are you Juan's sister?)

Ana: Hola, el gusto es mío. Sí, soy la hermana de Juan, ¿lo conoces? (Hi, the pleasure is mine. Yes, I am Juan's sister. Do you know him?)

Javier: Sí, claro. Siempre estudiamos en la biblioteca de la escuela. (Yes, of course. We always study in the school library.)

Ana: ¡Qué interesante! Él es muy buen estudiante. (How interesting! He is a very good student.)

Javier: Sí, ¡lo es! Y está muy interesado en aprender a tocar un instrumento musical. (Yes, he is. And he is very interested in learning to play a musical instrument.)

Ana: Sí. (Yes.)

Javier: ¿Qué está haciendo ahora? (What is he doing now?)

Ana: En este momento él está en casa. (At this moment he is at home.)

Javier: ¿Está estudiando? (Is he studying?)

Ana: Sí, probablemente. (Yes, probably.)

Answer key:

> *Alberto: Hola, Javier ¿Cómo **estás**?* (Hi, Javier, how are you?)
>
> *Javier: Muy bien, ¿y tú?, Alberto.* (Very well, and you, Alberto?)
>
> *Alberto: Bien, gracias. Te presento a mi amiga Ana.* (Well, thank you. This is my friend Ana.)
>
> *Javier: Mucho gusto, Ana ¿**Eres** la hermana de Juan?* (Nice to meet you, Ana. Are you Juan's sister?)
>
> *Ana: Hola, el gusto **es** mío. Sí, **soy** la hermana de Juan, ¿lo conoces?* (Hi, the pleasure is mine. Yes, I am Juan's sister. Do you know him?)
>
> *Javier: Sí, claro. Siempre estudiamos en la biblioteca de la escuela.* (Yes, of course. We always study in the school library.)
>
> *Ana: ¡Qué interesante! Él **es** muy buen estudiante.* (How interesting! He is a very good student.)
>
> *Javier: Sí, ¡lo **es** ! Y **está** muy interesado en aprender a tocar un instrumento musical.* (Yes, he is. And he is very interested in learning to play a musical instrument.)
>
> *Ana: Sí.* (Yes.)
>
> *Javier: ¿Qué **está** haciendo ahora?* (What is he doing now?)
>
> *Ana: En este momento él **está** en casa.* (At this moment he is at home.)
>
> *Javier: ¿**Está** estudiando?* (Is he studying?)
>
> *Ana: Sí, probablemente.* (Yes, probably.)

¿De Dónde Eres? – Where Are You From?

The verb *ser* can help us to talk about where we're from. To say where you are from, use **ser (conjugated)** + *de* + **(country's name)**.

Practice: Read the story. Can you identify the sentences that use the verb **ser**?

Listen to Track 95

Hola, mi nombre es Pedro. Soy de Argentina, aunque mis padres son de Portugal. Tenemos algunas costumbres en casa de ese país, y en la escuela observo las de mi país, Argentina. Mi profesora de francés es de Francia, así que conozco varios idiomas. Tengo una vida muy interesante.

Answer key:

*Hola, mi nombre **es** Pedro.*
***Soy** de Argentina, aunque mis padres **son** de Portugal.*
*Mi profesora de francés **es** de Francia.*

Listen to Track 96

Practice: Answer the questions based on the story above.

1. *¿De dónde es Pedro?* (Where is Pedro from?)

   ____

2. *¿De dónde son sus padres?* (Where are his parents from?)

   ____

3. *¿De dónde es su profesora de francés?* (Where is his French teacher from?)

   ____

Answer key:

1. *Pedro es de Argentina.* (Pedro is from Argentina.)
2. *Sus padres son de Portugal.* (His parents are from Portugal.)
3. *Su profesora de francés es de Francia.* (His French teacher is from France.)

Here are some other ways to ask where someone is from:

Listen to Track 97

*¿De dónde **eres**?* (Where are **you** from?)
*¿De dónde **es él/ella**?* (Where is **he/she** from?)
*¿De dónde **es Susan**?* (Where is **Susan** from?)
*¿De dónde **es usted**?* (Where are **you** from?) (**polite**)
*¿De dónde **son ustedes**?* (Where are **you** from?) (**polite, plural**)
*¿De dónde **son ellos/ellas**?* (Where are **they** from?)

Practice: In groups of three, ask each other where you are from and share your nationality and *gentilicio*. Follow the example above.

La Comunidad – The Community

Listen to Track 98

Practice: Use a dictionary to relate the Spanish words with the English words in the table.

Spanish words bank:

la tienda - el taller - la capital - el bombero - la oficina - la universidad - la escuela - el hospital - la doctora - la granja - el hombre de negocios - el comerciante - el restaurante - la estación de bomberos - el mercado - la mesera - el mecánico - el cocinero - el presidente - el empleado

English	Spanish
businessman/ businesswoman	
shop	
capital	
hospital	
nurse	
doctor	
cook	
mechanic	
school	
university	
market	
office	
business owner/ merchant	
firefighter	
garage/workshop	
farm	
president	
waitress	
employee	
restaurant	
teacher	

Answers:

English	Spanish
businessman/ businesswoman	*el hombre de negocios / la mujer de negocios*
shop/store	*la tienda*
capital	*la capital*
hospital	*el hospital*
nurse	*la enfermera / el enfermero*
doctor	*la doctora / el doctor*
cook	*el cocinero / la cocinera*
mechanic	*el mecánico / la mecánico*
school	*la escuela*
university	*la universidad*
market	*el mercado*
office	*la oficina*
business owner/merchant	*el comerciante / la comerciante*
firefighter	*el bombero / la bombero*
garage/workshop	*el taller*
farm	*la granja*
president	*el presidente / la presidenta*
waitress	*la mesera / el mesero*
employee	*el empleado / la empleada*
restaurant	*el restaurante*
teacher	*el maestro / la maestra / el profesor / la profesora*

Listen to Track 99

Practice: Write the correct conjugation of the verbs *trabajar* (to work) or *ser* (to be) in the blanks. Use the verb *ser* for professions and the verb *trabajar* for places.

Yo _________ en un hospital. Yo _________ un doctor.	Yo _________ en una oficina. Yo ____ un hombre de negocios.
Nosotros _________ en la estación de bomberos. Nosotros _________ bomberos.	Nosotros ___________ en un taller. Nosotros _________ mecánicos.
Ella _________ en una oficina. Ella ___ una empleada.	Él _________ en un mercado. Él ____ un comerciante.
Él _________ en un restaurante. Él ___ un cocinero.	Usted _________ en la universidad. Usted ____ un profesor.
Ellas _________ en una escuela. Ellas ____ maestras.	Él _________ en la residencia presidencial. Él ___ el presidente.

Answers:

Yo *trabajo* en un hospital. Yo *soy* un doctor.	Yo *trabajo* en una oficina. Yo *soy* un hombre de negocios.
Nosotros *trabajamos* en la estación de bomberos. Nosotros *somos* bomberos.	Nosotros *trabajamos* en un taller. Nosotros *somos* mecánicos.
Ella *trabaja* en una oficina. Ella *es* una empleada.	Él *trabaja* en un mercado. Él *es* un comerciante.
Él *trabaja* en un restaurante. Él *es* un cocinero.	Usted *trabaja* en la universidad. Usted *es* un profesor.
Ellas *trabajan* en una escuela. Ellas *son* maestras.	Él *trabaja* en la residencia presidencial. Él *es* el presidente.

"Usar" O "Llevar Puesto" – To Wear Clothes

In Spanish, we say *"usar"* or *"llevar puesto"* when we want to talk about the clothes we are wearing. Here's how to conjugate *usar* (to use) and *llevar* (to carry/bring):

Listen to Track 100

Subject	*usar* (to use)	*llevar* (to carry/bring)
Yo	*uso*	*llevo*
Tú	*usas*	*llevas*
Él, ella, usted	*usa*	*lleva*
Vos	*usás*	*llevás*
Vosotros, vosotras	*usáis*	*lleváis*
Nosotros, nosotras	*usamos*	*llevamos*
Ustedes	*usan*	*llevan*
Ellos, ellas	*usan*	*llevan*

The words *llevar* and *puesto* each have several different meanings on their own, depending on context. But together, *llevar puesto* means "to wear."

As an adjective, *puesto* needs to agree in gender and number with the noun it modifies, the noun in this case being the clothing item.

Listen to Track 101

For example: **el** *sombrero* → *Llevo pues***to un** *sombrero.*
la *chaqueta* → *Llevo pues***ta una** *chaqueta.*
los *zapatos* → *Llevo pues***tos unos** *zapatos.*
las *sandalias* → *Llevo pues***tas unas** *sandalias.*

Here is a list of clothes you can wear.

Listen to Track 102

el vestido (dress)
el sombrero (hat)
las botas (boots)
la chaqueta (jacket)
el suéter (sweater)

los pantalones (pants)
la camisa (shirt)
el abrigo (coat)
los zapatos (shoes)
las sandalias (sandals)

Listen to Track 103

Practice: *¿Qué llevas puesto?* (What are you wearing?)

Translate the English sentences to Spanish. For every English sentence, make two Spanish sentences using **usar** *and* **llevar puesto**.

1. Carolina wears a dress.

   Carolina <u>usa</u> un vestido.
   Carolina <u>lleva puesto</u> un vestido.

2. The boys wear sandals.

3. You (*tú*) wear the jacket.

4. I wear a coat.

5. We wear boots.

6. You (*usted*) wear a sweater.

Answers:

2. The boys wear sandals.

   Los niños <u>usan</u> unas sandalias.
   Los niños <u>llevan puestas</u> unas sandalias.

3. You (*tú*) wear the jacket.

   (Tú) <u>Usas</u> la chaqueta.
   (Tú) <u>Llevas puesta</u> la chaqueta.

4. I wear a coat.

   (Yo) <u>Uso</u> un abrigo.
   (Yo) <u>Llevo puesto</u> un abrigo.

5. We wear boots.

   Nosotros/nosotras <u>usamos</u> unas botas.
   Nosotros/nosotras <u>llevamos puestas</u> unas botas.

6. You (*usted*) wear a sweater.

   Usted <u>usa</u> un suéter.
   Usted <u>lleva puesta</u> un suéter.

"Ponerse" – To Put On

If *usar* and *llevar puesto* are used to talk about clothes we are wearing, we use **ponerse** to talk about putting on clothes.

ponerse (to put on [oneself])

Poner is a pronominal verb, which is why you see the *-se* at the end of its infinitive verb form. As such, we can add reflexive pronouns: **me, te, se, nos,** or **os**. This helps to clarify who is putting the clothes on, and who the clothes are being put on, in case they happen to be different (like a mother putting clothes on her child).

Here's how to conjugate the verb *ponerse* in the simple present tense. Remember to include the reflexive pronouns: **me, te, se, nos,** or **os**.

Listen to Track 104

Subject	*ponerse* (to put on [oneself])
Yo	me pongo
Tú	te pones
Él, ella, usted	se pone
Vos	os ponés
Vosotros, vosotras	os ponéis
Nosotros, nosotras	nos ponemos
Ustedes	se ponen
Ellos, ellas	se ponen

Listen to Track 105

Practice: Fill in the blanks with the appropriate conjugated form of *ponerse*.

Carlos **se** __________ el sombrero en las mañanas.	(Carlos puts on his hat in the morning.)
Los niños **se** __________ los zapatos.	(The children put on their shoes.)
Yo **le** __________ un collar a mi perro.	(I put a collar on my dog.)

Answers:

1. *se pone*
2. *se ponen*
3. *le pongo*

"Jugar" Vs. *"Tocar"* – To Play

In English, you can play games, and you can play musical instruments. However, in Spanish, we have two different verbs for playing:

Listen to Track 106

tocar *un instrumento* (to play an instrument) Examples: *tocar el piano, la guitarra, la batería, el violín,* etc.
jugar *un juego* (to play a game, sports) Example: *jugar al fútbol.*

Examples: *Juguemos al fútbol.* (Let's play soccer.)
Tocamos la guitarra. (Let's play the guitar.)
Juguemos al tenis. (Let's play tennis.)

Jugar and *tocar* are both irregular verbs, so the root is subject to change with the conjugations. Here's how to conjugate **jugar** (to play) and **tocar** (to play):

Listen to Track 107

Subject	*jugar* (to play)	*tocar* (to play)
Yo	*juego*	*toco*
Tú	*juegas*	*tocas*
Él, ella, usted	*juega*	*toca*
Vos	*jugás*	*tocás*
Vosotros, vosotras	*jugáis*	*tocáis*
Nosotros, nosotras	*jugamos*	*tocamos*
Ustedes	*juegan*	*tocan*
Ellos, ellas	*juegan*	*tocan*

Listen to Track 108

Practice: Complete the sentences using the correct conjugated verb: *jugar* or *tocar*.

Note: After the verb *jugar* we can use *a/al*. But you can choose to not use them, and it will still be grammatically correct.

1. *Susan _____________ el piano.*
2. *Tú ___________ al fútbol.*
3. *Ellos ____________ violín.*
4. *Daniel _____________ tenis con sus amigos.*
5. *Los niños ________________ en el parque.*

Answers:

1. *Susan <u>toca</u> el piano.*
2. *Tú <u>juegas</u> al fútbol.*
3. *Ellos <u>tocan</u> violín.*
4. *Daniel <u>juega</u> tenis con sus amigos.*
5. *Los niños <u>juegan</u> en el parque.*

Practice: Read the paragraph below and then write next to each statement *verdadero* if it is true and *falso* if it is false.

Listen to Track 109

*En México nos gustan mucho los deportes. Especialmente el fútbol que es muy popular. Todos los niños aprenden a **jugar** fútbol y otros deportes en la escuela. También es común hacer competencias y **juegos** entre diferentes escuelas. En México le llaman fútbol a lo que en los Estados Unidos le llaman soccer y le dicen fútbol americano a lo que en Estados Unidos le llaman fútbol. El fútbol americano no es muy popular en México y casi no hay equipos profesionales. Por otro lado, hay muchos **equipos** profesionales de fútbol.*	(In Mexico, we like sports very much. Especially soccer, which is very popular. All children learn to **play** soccer and other sports at school. It is also common to arrange competitions and **matches** between different schools. In Mexico, we call football what people in the United States call soccer, and we call American football what people in the United States call football. American football is not very popular in Mexico and there are almost no professional teams. On the other hand, there are many professional soccer **teams**.)

Listen to Track 110

Verdadero/Falso

En México les gustan mucho los deportes. _____________

El fútbol no es popular en México. _____________

Los niños aprenden deportes en la escuela. _____________

Es común hacer competencias entre escuelas. _____________

El fútbol americano es muy popular en México. _____________

Hay muchos equipos profesionales de fútbol. _____________

Answers:

1. *Verdadero*	3. *Verdadero*	5. *Falso*
2. *Falso*	4. *Verdadero*	6. *Verdadero*

Listen to Track 111

Practice: Answer the following questions with *sí* (yes) or *no* (no).

sí/no

1. *¿Te gustan los deportes?* ____
2. *¿En tu escuela practican deportes?* ____
3. *¿Has participado en una competencia de deportes?* ____

Verbos Que Terminan en "-Er" – Verbs Ending in "-Er"

All regular verbs that finish with *-er* have the same ending when conjugated. Follow the same rules you learn with verbs ending in *-ar*:

Find the infinitive form of a verb ending with *-er*.

Replace the *-er* ending with the conjugation according to the subject and tense.

These are the endings for each subject in the simple present tense:

Listen to Track 112

Subject	Ending	*leer* (to read)
Yo	-o	leo
Tú	-es	lees
Vos	-és	leés
Él, ella, usted	-e	lee
Nosotros, nosotras	-emos	leemos
Vosotros, vosotras	-éis	leéis
Ustedes	-en	leen
Ellos, ellas	-en	leen

Practice: Write the correct conjugation of the following regular verbs:

Subject	*comer* (to eat)	*correr* (to run)	*aprender* (to learn)	*responder* (to respond)
Yo				
Tú				
Vos				
Él, ella, usted				
Nosotros/as				
Vosotros/as				
Ustedes				
Ellos, ellas				

Listen to Track 113

Answers:

Subject	comer (to eat)	correr (to run)	aprender (to learn)	responder (to respond)
Yo	como	corro	aprendo	respondo
Tú	comes	corres	aprendes	respondes
Vos	comés	corrés	aprendés	respondés
Él, ella, usted	come	corre	aprende	responde
Nosotros/as	comemos	corremos	aprendemos	respondemos
Vosotros/as	coméis	corréis	aprendéis	respondéis
Ustedes	comen	corren	aprenden	responden
Ellos, ellas	comen	corren	aprenden	responden

There are other useful regular *-er* verbs:

Listen to Track 114

beber (to drink)	barrer (to sweep)	comprender (to understand)	ver (to see)

Write the following sentences in Spanish:

English	Spanish
He drinks.	
I understand.	
We see.	Nosotros
You sweep.	Ustedes
They run.	Ellos
You eat.	Vosotros
You answer.	Tú
She reads.	

Listen to Track 115

Answers:

English	Spanish
He drinks.	*Él bebe.*
I understand.	*Yo comprendo.*
We see.	*Nosotros vemos.*
You sweep.	*Ustedes barren.*
They run.	*Ellos corren.*
You eat.	*Vosotros coméis.*
You answer.	*Tú respondes.*
She reads.	*Ella lee.*

Verbos Que Terminan en "-Ir" – Verbs Ending in "-Ir"

Regular verbs that finish with *-ir* follow the same rules and patterns as verbs that finish with *-ar* or verbs that finish with *-er*. You just need to learn the correct endings for *-ir* verbs.

These are the endings for each subject in the simple present tense:

Listen to Track 116

Subject	Ending	*decidir* (to decide)
Yo	*-o*	*decido*
Tú	*-es*	*decides*
Vos	*-ís*	*decidís*
Él, ella, usted	*-e*	*decide*
Nosotros, nosotras	*-imos*	*decidimos*
Vosotros, vosotras	*-ís*	*decidís*
Ustedes	*-en*	*deciden*
Ellos, ellas	*-en*	*deciden*

The endings for verbs that finish with *-ir* are almost the same as for the verbs that finish with *-er*. Only the subjects *vos, vosotros/as,* and *nosotros/as* change.

Repaso De Los Verbos – Verb Review

<u>**Listen to Track 117**</u>

Match the Spanish verbs in the infinitive form to their English equivalent below:

to print	to draw	to jump	to eat	to run
to comprehend	to open	to walk	to cover	to share
to learn	to sing	to feed		

1. *alimentar* _______________________________
2. *caminar* _______________________________
3. *cantar* _______________________________
4. *dibujar* _______________________________
5. *saltar* _______________________________
6. *aprender* _______________________________
7. *comer* _______________________________
8. *comprender* _______________________________
9. *correr* _______________________________
10. *abrir* _______________________________
11. *compartir* _______________________________
12. *cubrir* _______________________________
13. *imprimir* _______________________________

Answers:

1. *alimentar* — to feed
2. *caminar* — to walk
3. *cantar* — to sing
4. *dibujar* — to draw
5. *saltar* — to jump
6. *aprender* — to learn
7. *comer* — to eat
8. *comprender* — to comprehend
9. *correr* — to run
10. *abrir* — to open
11. *compartir* — to share
12. *cubrir* — to cover
13. *imprimir* — to print

Usando Los Verbos – Using Verbs

Let's review how to conjugate regular verbs ending with *-ar*, *-er*, and *-ir*. When we conjugate regular verbs in the present tense, their endings are replaced with:

Listen to Track 118

Subject	*-ar*	*-er*	*-ir*
Yo	*o*	*o*	*o*
Tú	*as*	*es*	*es*
Él, ella, usted	*a*	*e*	*e*
Nosotros, nosotras	*amos*	*emos*	*imos*
Vos	*ás*	*és*	*ís*
Vosotros, vosotras	*áis*	*éis*	*ís*
Ustedes	*an*	*en*	*en*
Ellos, ellas	*an*	*en*	*en*

Listen to Track 119

Practice: Complete the sentences with the conjugated verb in the present tense.

1. *Rosa* _____________ *(caminar) en el parque.* (Rosa walks in the park.)
2. *Los niños* _____________ *(cantar).* (The kids sing.)
3. *Caroline* _____________ *(dibujar) un paisaje.* (Caroline draws a landscape.)
4. *David* _________ *(saltar) la cuerda muy bien.* (David jumps rope very well.)
5. *Luisa* _____________ *(correr) en la competencia.* (Luisa runs in the competition.)
6. *Joseph* _____________ *(comer) en el restaurante.* (Joseph eats in the restaurant.)
7. *Carlos* _____________ *(aprender) a tocar piano.* (Carlos learns to play the piano.)
8. *Diana* _____________ *las hojas.* (Diana prints the sheets.)
9. *Mis padres* _____________ *el almuerzo.* (My parents share lunch.)

Answers:

1. *camina*
2. *cantan*
3. *dibuja*
4. *salta*
5. *corre*
6. *come*
7. *aprende*
8. *imprime*
9. *comparten*

Here are some common Spanish verbs ending in *-er* and *-ir*.

-er verbs:

Listen to Track 120

comer	(to eat)
correr	(to run)
temer	(to fear)
vender	(to sell)

Practice: Write a sentence with the verb *comer*. Choose a subject or personal pronoun: *yo, tú, él, ella, nosotros, nosotras, vos, vosotros, vosotras, ustedes, ellos, ellas.*

Example:

Manuel come en el restaurante de la familia de Lili todos los días.	(Manuel eats at Lili's family's restaurant every day.)

Practice: Write more sentences with the verbs *correr, temer,* and *vender.*

correr:	
temer:	
vender:	

Listen to Track 121

Sample answers: *Corro a la escuela.* (I run to school.)
Temo los exámenes. (I dread exams.)
Vendemos libros en linea. (We sell books online.)

Listen to Track 122

-ir verbs:

decidir	(to decide)
escribir	(to write)
vivir	(to live)
abrir	(to open)

Practice: Write sentences with the verbs above.

decidir:	
escribir:	
vivir:	
abrir:	

Listen to Track 123

Sample answers: *Ella decide comprar helado.* (She decides to buy ice cream.)
Están escribiendo un ensayo. (They are writing an essay.)
¡Vivamos en Hawái! (Let's live in Hawaii!)
No abra el frasco de galletas. (Don't open the cookie jar.)

To negate a sentence in Spanish, we just add the word "*no*" before the conjugated verb. This means that the subject is **not** doing the action.

Listen to Track 124

Examples: *No quiero ir al parque.* (I do not want to go to the park.)
Alejandro no come frutas. (Alejandro does not eat fruits.)
Sheyla no va a la biblioteca. (Sheyla does not go to the library.)
¿Por qué no juegas con Ana? (Why don't you play with Ana?)

Practice: Negate the sentences.

1. *David lee el libro.* (David reads the book.)

____

2. *Alex y Roberto comen helados.* (Alex and Roberto eat ice cream.)

____

3. *Rodrigo va a la fiesta.* (Rodrigo goes to the party.)

____

4. *Mi familia come frutas.* (My family eats fruits.)

____

5. *Anita tiene un reloj.* (Anita has a watch.)

____

Listen to Track 125

Answers:

1. *David <u>no</u> lee el libro.* (David does not read the book.)
2. *Alex y Roberto <u>no</u> comen helados.* (Alex and Roberto do not eat ice cream.)
3. *Rodrigo <u>no</u> va a la fiesta.* (Rodrigo does not go to the party.)
4. *Mi familia <u>no</u> come frutas.* (My family does not eat fruit.)
5. *Anita <u>no</u> tiene un reloj.* (Anita does not have a watch.)

Practice: Make your own negative sentences with the following verbs. Remember to write "*no*" before the verb, as shown in negative sentences in this chapter.

comprar: (to buy)	
beber: (to drink)	
cantar: (to sing)	

"Tener" – To Have

We use the verb *tener* to express possession of tangible and intangible elements. *Tener* is an irregular verb, so the root *ten-* is subject to change, depending on the conjugated form.

Listen to Track 126

Subject	*tener* (to have)
Yo	*tengo*
Tú	*tienes*
Él, ella, usted	*tiene*
Vos	*tenés*
Vosotros, vosotras	*tenéis*
Nosotros, nosotras	*tenemos*
Ustedes	*tienen*
Ellos, ellas	*tienen*

Listen to Track 127

Practice: Answer the questions in Spanish.

1. *¿Tienes muchos libros?* (Do you have many books?)

____

2. *¿Tu casa tiene un techo rojo?* (Does your house have a red roof?)

____

3. *¿Ana tiene muchos amigos?* (Does Ana have many friends?)

____

Answers:

1. *Sí, tengo muchos libros.* (Yes, I have many books.)
2. *Sí, mi casa tiene un techo rojo.* (Yes, my house has a red roof.)
3. *Sí, Ana tiene muchos amigos.* (Yes, Ana has many friends.)

Otros Usos de "Tener" – Other Uses of "To Have"

"Tener" is used in many Spanish phrases and expressions, including:

Listen to Track 128

A. When feeling hot or cold: *tener calor/frío.*

*David **tiene** mucho **frío**.*	(David is very cold.)
*En el invierno, nosotros **tenemos** calor.*	(In the summer, we are hot.)

B. When describing age: *tener _____ años.*

*El abuelito de Lucy **tiene** 80 **años**.*	(Lucy's grandfather is 80 years old.)

C. When feeling hungry, thirsty, or tired: *tener hambre/sed/sueño.*

*El niño **tiene hambre**.*	(The boy is hungry.)
*¿**Tienes sed**? Necesitas agua.*	(Feeling thirsty? You need water.)
*El bebé **tiene sueño**.*	(The baby is tired/sleepy.)

Listen to Track 129

Practice: Fill in the blanks with the correct usage and conjugation of *tener*.

1. They're playing soccer, so they are thirsty.
   Ellos juegan al fútbol, así que __________ __________.
2. David is in the restaurant and is very hungry.
   David está en el restaurante y __________ mucha __________.
3. Lucas is very sleepy.
   Lucas __________ mucho __________.
4. Alejandro is 5 years old and José is 8 years old.
   Alejandro __________ 5 __________ y José 8 __________.

Answers:

1. *Ellos juegan al fútbol, así que **tienen** sed.*
2. *David está en el restaurante y **tiene** mucha hambre.*
3. *Lucas **tiene** mucho sueño.*
4. *Alejandro **tiene** 5 años y José 8 años.*

Some other uses of *tener* (to have) include:

Listen to Track 130

D. When someone is right or wrong: *tener razón / no tener razón.*

Tienes razón, mi carro es viejo.	You are right, my car is old.
No tienen razón, yo no trabajo aquí.	They are wrong, I don't work here.

E. When feeling afraid:

Listen to Track 131

tener miedo de + (infinitive verb) = afraid to do an action

tener miedo a + (noun) = afraid of something

Tengo miedo a la oscuridad.	I'm afraid of the dark.
Ella tiene miedo de salir.	She is afraid to go outside.

F. When lucky: *tener suerte*

Tienes suerte de estudiar aquí.	You are lucky to study here.

G. When successful: *tener éxito*

Ella tiene mucho éxito en su negocio.	She is very successful with her business.

H. When careful: *tener cuidado*

Ten cuidado con la bicicleta.	Be careful with the bicycle.

Listen to Track 132

Practice: Answer the questions with complete sentences.

1. *¿De qué tienes suerte?* ________________________
2. *¿A qué le tienes miedo?* ________________________
3. *¿Cuántos años tienes?* ________________________
4. *¿Tienes cuidado con los coches?* ________________________
5. *¿Tiene éxito tu mamá?* ________________________

Sample answers:

1. *¿De qué tienes suerte?* — *Tengo suerte de estudiar español.*
2. *¿A qué le tienes miedo?* — *Le tengo miedo a los doctores.*
3. *¿Cuántos años tienes?* — *Tengo 15 años.*
4. *¿Tienes cuidado con los coches?* — *Sí, yo tengo cuidado con los coches.*
5. *¿Tiene éxito tu mamá?* — *Sí, mi mamá tiene éxito en su trabajo.*

When we express an obligation, we use the verb *tener* conjugated in the present tense followed by *que*.

Listen to Track 133

Example: ***Tengo que*** *estudiar mi lección de Historia.*

Notice that the subject pronoun for *tener* is not included in this sentence, but implied by the conjugation of the verb *tener: yo tengo.*

Listen to Track 134

Practice: Fill in the blanks with the correct conjugation of *tener.*

1. ______________________ *que trabajar en la tarde.*
   (I have to work in the afternoon.)
2. *Los niños* ______________________ *que guardar los juguetes.*
   (The children have to put away the toys.)
3. *Mi papá* ______________________ *que culminar sus estudios.*
   (My dad has to finish his studies.)
4. *Nosotras* ______________________ *que limpiar nuestra casa en la tarde.*
   (We have to clean our house in the afternoon.)
5. *Mari* ______________________ *que entregar sus tareas a tiempo en la escuela.*
   (Mari has to turn in her homework on time at school.)
6. *Mis amigos* ______________________ *que ayudar a sus padres todos los días.*
   (My friends have to help their parents every day.)

Answers:

1. *Tengo que trabajar en la tarde.*
2. *Los niños tienen que guardar los juguetes.*
3. *Mi papá tiene que culminar sus estudios.*
4. *Nosotras tenemos que limpiar nuestra casa en la tarde.*
5. *Mari tiene que entregar sus tareas a tiempo en la escuela.*
6. *Mis amigos tienen que ayudar a sus padres todos los días.*

Listen to Track 135

Practice: Make sentences with *tener que* from the following expressions. The first exercise has been done for you.

1. *Llegar temprano a la escuela. (Tú)*   *Tienes que llegar temprano a la escuela.*
   (Arrive early to school.)

2. *Comer su desayuno. (Usted)*   ______________________________
   (Eat your breakfast.)

3. *Ayudar a sus padres. (Ellos)*   ______________________________
   (Help her parents.

4. *Ir al supermercado. (Nosotros)*   ______________________________
   (Go to the supermarket.)

Answers: 2. *Usted tiene que comer su desayuno.*
   3. *Ellos tienen que ayudar a sus padres.*
   4. *Nosotros tenemos que ir al supermercado.*

Listen to Track 136

Practice: Write the Spanish sentences in the correct space to complete the chart.

Tengo mucha hambre.
Yo tengo cuidado con el perro.
No tienes razón.
Ella tiene ocho años.

¿A qué le tienes miedo?
Tengo los pies fríos.
Ellos tienen calor.
No tengo sueño.

English	Spanish
You are wrong.	
I am very hungry.	
She is eight years old.	
I am careful with the dog.	
They are hot.	
I have cold feet.	
What are you afraid of?	
We are not sleepy.	

Answers:

English	Spanish
You are not right.	*No tienes razón.*
I am very hungry.	*Tengo mucha hambre.*
She is eight years old.	*Ella tiene ocho años.*
I am careful with the dog.	*Yo tengo cuidado con el perro.*
They are hot.	*Ellos tienen calor.*
I have cold feet.	*Tengo los pies fríos.*
What are you afraid of?	*¿A qué le tienes miedo?*
We are not sleepy.	*No tenemos sueño.*

Listen to Track 137

Practice: Complete the sentences.

1. *Encontré un billete de cinco dólares en la calle. Tengo mucha* ______________.
   (I found a five-dollar bill in the street. I'm very lucky.)

2. *No desayuné. Tengo mucha* ____________________.
   (I didn't have breakfast. I'm very hungry.)

3. *No hay ni una nube y estamos en verano. Tengo mucho* ______________.
   (There are no clouds and it is summer. I'm very hot.)

4. *No quiero ir a la playa. Le tengo* _________ *al mar.*
   (I don't want to go to the beach. I'm afraid of the sea.)

Answers:

1. *Encontré un billete de cinco dólares en la calle. Tengo mucha <u>suerte</u>.*
2. *No desayuné. Tengo mucha <u>hambre</u>.*
3. *No hay ni una nube y estamos en verano. Tengo mucho <u>calor</u>.*
4. *No quiero ir a la playa. Le tengo <u>miedo</u> al mar.*

"Más Que" – More Than

We use **más que** to make comparisons. The word *más* means more, and can be used to compare qualities and quantities.

Listen to Track 138

For example: *Santiago tiene **tres** lápices.* (Santiago has **three** pencils.)
*Mari tiene **un** lápiz.* (Mari has **one** pencil.)

*Santiago tiene **más** lápices **que** Mari.*
(Santiago has **more** pencils **than** Mari.)

Listen to Track 139

Practice: Consider how quantitative *más...que* statements are made, based on the example above. Fill in the blanks with *más...que* (more...than) where appropriate in these expressions about quantities.

1. *Lucy compra_________ pizzas_______ Ale.* (Lucy buys more pizzas than Ale.)
2. *Ana canta_______ canciones_______ Luis.* (Ana sings more songs than Luis.)
3. *Julia come _______ helados ______ Juan.* (Julia eats more ice cream than Juan.)

Answers:

1. *Lucy compra **más** pizzas **que** Ale.*
2. *Ana canta **más** canciones **que** Luis.*
3. *Julia come **más** helados **que** Juan.*

The expression *más que* can also be used to compare qualities with adjectives or adverbs. Notice that in English, we say bigger, or faster, but in Spanish, they say *más grande* ("more big"), or *más rapido* ("more fast"), etc.

Listen to Track 140

Practice: Write these sentences in Spanish using the vocabulary provided below and from previous chapters of the book! The first question has been answered for you.

1. The shoes are uglier ("more ugly") than the hat.   (*feo* = ugly)
   *Los zapatos son **más** feo **que** el sombrero.*

2. My coat is bigger ("more big") than your coat.   (*grande* = big)

   ____

3. You run faster ("more fast") than me.   (*rápido* = fast)

   ____

4. Ana is prettier ("more pretty") than her cat.   (*bonito/bonita* = pretty)
   (*el gato* = cat)

   ____

Answers:

2. *Mi abrigo es **más** grande **que** tu abrigo.*
3. *(Tu) Corres **más** rápido **que** yo.*
4. *Ana es **más** bonita **que** su gato.*

"Menos Que" – Less Than, Fewer Than

We use *más que* to say "more than," and **menos que** to say "less than" or "fewer than." The word *menos* means "less," and like the word *más*, is used with adjectives, adverbs, and nouns to compare their qualities and quantities. Don't forget that adjectives need to agree in gender and number with the nouns they modify!

Examples of comparing quantities:

Listen to Track 141

Mis amigos tienen <u>menos</u> juguetes <u>que</u> mis primos.
(My friends have <u>fewer</u> toys <u>than</u> my cousins.)

Lucy pinta <u>menos</u> cuadros <u>que</u> Mari.
(Lucy paints <u>fewer</u> pictures <u>than</u> Mari.)

Example of comparing qualities:

Lili es <u>menos</u> amigable <u>que</u> su hermana.
(Lili is <u>less</u> friendly <u>than</u> her sister.)

Las matemáticas son <u>menos</u> difíciles <u>que</u> la física.
(Math is <u>less</u> difficult <u>than</u> physics.)

Listen to Track 142

Practice: Write your own sentences using the negative comparison **menos...que.** Use the above examples from this chapter and the *más...que* chapter to model your own sentences after.

Sample answers: *Mi prima es menos alta que mi abuela.*
(My cousin is shorter than my grandmother.)

Luis tiene menos suerte que yo.
(Luis is less lucky than me.)

____

____

____

We use **tan…como** (as…as) to express equal comparisons in qualities (adverbs, adjectives) between objects, people, and situations.

Listen to Track 143

For example: *Lucía obtiene buenas notas.* (Lucía gets good grades.)
Karla también. (Karla, too.)
*Lucía es **tan** inteligente **como** Karla.* (Lucía is as smart as Karla.)

David es muy famoso. (David is very famous.)
Lucas también. (Lucas, too.)
*David es **tan** famoso **como** Lucas.* (Davis is as famous as Lucas.)

Listen to Track 144

Practice: Make your own sentences expressing equality using *tan…como* using the following adjectives. Remember that adjectives need to agree in gender and number with the noun they modify!

juguetón/-ona = playful   *bajo/-a* = short   *talentoso/-a* = talented

____

____

____

Listen to Track 145

While we use *tan…como* to express equal qualities (adjectives and adverbs), we use **tanto…como** (as…as) to express equal quantities (nouns) between plural objects, situations, characteristics, animals or persons. *Tanto* needs to agree with the noun it goes before in gender and number.

Examples: *Cocinar lleva <u>tanto</u> tiempo <u>como</u> comer.*
(Cooking takes as much time as eating.)

Los niños tienen <u>tantos</u> libros <u>como</u> la profesora.
(The boys have as many books as the teacher.)

Mi hermana escucha <u>tanta</u> música <u>como</u> nuestros padres.
(My sister listens to as much music as our parents.)

Laura canta <u>tantas</u> canciones <u>como</u> Jorge.
(Laura sings as many songs as Jorge.)

Practice: Write your own sentences using the expression ***tanto...como.*** Use the above examples to model your own answers after.

Sample answer: *Tengo <u>tantas</u> sandalias <u>como</u> Erin.*
(I have as many sandals as Erin.)

____

____

____

Las Comparaciones – Comparisons

For comparisons, there are some adjectives and adverbs that don't use the words *más* and *menos*. They use a unique form for comparisons.

Listen to Track 146

Adjectives	
Spanish	**English**
mucho - más	much - more
poco - menos	little - less
bueno - mejor	good - better
malo - peor	bad - worse
grande - mayor	old - older
pequeño - menor	young - younger

Adverbs	
Spanish	**English**
mucho - más	much - more
poco - menos	little - less
bien - mejor	well - better
mal - peor	badly - worse

The words *grande* and *pequeño* only change if they are talking about age. If they refer to size, use *más* and *menos*.

Listen to Track 147

*Mi hermano es **mayor** que yo.* (My brother is older than me.)
*Tú balón es más **grande** que el mío.* (Your ball is bigger than mine.)
*Tú lees más **rápido** que yo.* (You read faster than me.)
*Ana es **mejor** cocinera que tú.* (Ana is a better cook than you.)
*Él canta **peor** que lo que escribe.* (He sings worse than he writes.)

Practice: Write the following sentences in Spanish.

1. She has more dogs than him. ___________________________
2. He is worse at playing tennis than me. ___________________________
3. They work less than you. ___________________________
4. My brother is older than me. ___________________________

Listen to Track 148

Answers:

1. *Ella tiene más perros que él.*
2. *Él es peor jugando tenis que yo.*
3. *Ellos trabajan menos que tú.*
4. *Mi hermano es mayor que yo.*

Listen to Track 149

Practice: Write the sentences in Spanish. Use the vocabulary given.

1. My dog is bigger than yours. *(perro/grande/tuyo)*

    ____

2. He is as tall as a giraffe. *(él/alto/jirafa)*

    ____

3. We are hungrier than the dog. *(Nosotros/hambre/perro)*

    ____

4. The sun is brighter than the moon. *(sol/brillante/luna)*

    ____

5. Juan is as big as a bear. *(Juan/grande/oso)*

    ____

6. I don't have as much hair as you do. *(tengo/cabello/tú)*

    ____

7. She is less angry than you are. *(ella/enojada/tú)*

    ____

8. The car is larger than the bike. *(carro/grande/bici)*

    ____

Answers:

1. *Mi perro es más grande que el tuyo.*
2. *Él es tan alto como una jirafa.*
3. *Tenemos más hambre que el perro.*
4. *El sol es más brillante que la luna.*
5. *Juan es tan grande como un oso.*
6. *No tengo tanto cabello como tú.*
7. *Ella está menos enojada que tú.*
8. *El carro es más grande que la bici.*

"Querer" – To Want

Subject	*querer* (to want)
Yo	*quiero*
Tú	*quieres*
Él, ella, usted	*quiere*
Vos	*querés*
Vosotros, vosotras	*queréis*
Nosotros, nosotras	*queremos*
Ustedes	*quieren*
Ellos, ellas	*quieren*

Listen to Track 151

Practice: *¡Feliz cumpleaños!* (Happy birthday!)

Querer can be used to express the desire for an object. The formula to express this in Spanish is: **Subject + *querer* (conjugated) + noun + complement.**

So what do you want for your birthday? Write complete sentences in Spanish about what everyone wants. The first one has already been done for you.

1. *yo - una cámara de fotos* (I - a camera)*:*
   (yo) Quiero una cámara de fotos.

2. *tú - muchos regalos* (you - many presents)*:*
   ____

3. *el niño - una bicicleta* (the boy - a bicycle)*:*
   ____

4. *la abuela - una torta* (grandmother - a cake)*:*
   ____

5. *los gemelos - una computadora* (the twins - a computer)*:*
   ____

6. *usted - un libro* (you[formal] - a book)*:*
   ____

7. *mis hermanas - dos entradas para el concierto* (my sisters - two concert tickets)*:*
   ____

8. *nosotras - una casa nueva* (we[female] - a new house):

____

Answers:

1. <u>*(yo) Quiero una cámara de fotos.*</u>
2. <u>*(tú) Quieres muchos regalos.*</u>
3. <u>*El niño quiere una bicicleta.*</u>
4. <u>*La abuela quiere una torta.*</u>
5. <u>*Los gemelos quieren una computadora.*</u>
6. <u>*Usted quiere un libro.*</u>
7. <u>*Mis hermanas quieren dos entradas para el concierto.*</u>
8. <u>*Nosotras queremos una casa nueva.*</u>

Querer can also be used to express a desire for an action or activity. The formula to express this in Spanish is:

> **Subject + *querer* (conjugated) + verb (infinitive) + complement.**

Practice: Read the story below, and highlight the expressions using:

> ***querer* (conjugated) + verb (infinitive)**

Listen to Track 152

Marta, Lili y Beatriz planean ir al museo y se preguntan qué quieren hacer y llevar para disfrutar. (Marta, Lili, and Beatriz are planning to go to the museum and are wondering what they want to do and what to enjoy.)

Marta: Oye, Lili ¿qué quieres hacer en el museo? (Hey, Lili, what do you want to do at the museum?)

Lili: Quiero disfrutar viendo unas bonitas pinturas. (I want to enjoy looking at some nice paintings.)

Marta: ¿Ya reconoces algunas? (Do you already know some of them?)

Lili: Todavía no, por eso quiero ir. (Not yet. That's why I want to go.)

Marta: ¡Perfecto! Y tú, Beatriz ¿Qué quieres hacer en el museo? (Perfect! And you, Beatriz, what do you want to do at the museum?)

Beatriz: Yo quiero disfrutar viendo obras de arte modernas. (I want to enjoy looking at modern pieces of art.)

Marta: ¡Ok!, vamos todas a disfrutar. (Okay! Let's all go and enjoy ourselves.)

Answer key:

Marta, Lili y Beatriz planean ir al museo y se preguntan **qué quieren hacer y llevar para disfrutar**. (Marta, Lili, and Beatriz are planning to go to the museum and are wondering what they want to do and what to enjoy.)

Marta: Oye, Lili ¿qué **quieres hacer** *en el museo?* (Hey, Lili, what do you want to do at the museum?)

Lili: **Quiero disfrutar** *viendo unas bonitas pinturas.* (I want to enjoy looking at some nice paintings.)

Marta: ¿Ya reconoces algunas? (Do you already know some of them?)

Lili: Todavía no, por eso **quiero ir**. (Not yet. That's why I want to go.)

Marta: ¡Perfecto! Y tú, Beatriz ¿Qué **quieres hacer** *en el museo?* (Perfect! And you, Beatriz, what do you want to do at the museum?)

Beatriz: Yo **quiero disfrutar** *viendo obras de arte modernas.* (I want to enjoy looking at modern pieces of art.)

Marta: ¡Ok!, vamos todas a disfrutar. (Okay! Let's all go and enjoy ourselves.)

"Ir" – To Go

The verb **ir** is widely used in Spanish to express the action of moving somewhere.

Listen to Track 153

Subject	*ir* (to go)
Yo	*voy*
Tú	*vas*
Él, ella, usted	*va*
Vos	*vas*
Vosotros, vosotras	*vais*
Nosotros, nosotras	*vamos*
Ustedes	*van*
Ellos, ellas	*van*

Listen to Track 154

Practice: *¿A dónde van todos?* (Where is everyone going?)

Fill in the blanks with the conjugated *ir* to complete the sentences. The first question has already been done for you.

1. *Mis padres <u>van</u> al banco porque quieren dinero.*
   (My parents go to the bank because they want money.)
2. *(Yo) _____________ al parque porque quiero dar un paseo.*
   (I go to the park because I want to take a walk.)
3. *(Nosotros) _____________ al cine porque queremos ver una película.*
   (We go to the cinema because we want to watch a film.)
4. *¿(Tú) _____________ de compras? Sé que quieres una chaqueta blanca.*
   (Are you going shopping? I know that you want a white jacket.)
5. *Marc _____________ al supermercado porque él quiere comprar leche.*
   (Marc goes to the supermarket because he wants to buy some milk.)

Answers:

1. *Mis padres <u>van</u> al banco porque quieren dinero.*
2. *(Yo) <u>Voy</u> al parque porque quiero dar un paseo.*
3. *(Nosotros) <u>vamos</u> al cine porque queremos ver una película.*
4. *¿(Tú) <u>Vas</u> de compras? Sé que quieres una chaqueta blanca.*
5. *Marc <u>va</u> al supermercado porque quiere comprar leche.*

We can use *ir* (to go) to talk about a planned future action by using another verb in infinitive form. Don't forget the preposition **a** that goes between these two verbs! Follow this formula in Spanish.

> **Subject + *ir* (conjugated) + *a* + verb (infinitive)**

The English version of this would be **"I am going to" + verb (infinitive)**.

Listen to Track 155

Examples:　　*Voy a leer.* (I'm going to read.)
　　　　　　Vamos a estudiar. (We're going to study.)
　　　　　　Van a jugar. (They're going to play.)

Notice that we can actually omit a subject pronoun and still understand who we are talking about because of the way the verb *ir* is conjugated!

Listen to Track 156

Practice: Test your conjugation skills and change these simple sentences into a planned future action statement in Spanish. The first one has been done for you.

1. *Cantan en su casa.* (They sing at home.)
   <u>*Van a cantar en su casa.*</u> (They're going to sing at home.)

2. *Lees el documento.* (You read the document.)

   ____

3. *Él baila hoy.* (He dances today.)

   ____

4. *Visitamos a nuestros primos.* (We visit our cousins.)

   ____

5. *Bebo el café.* (I drink coffee.)

   ____

6. *Carla toca el piano.* (Carla plays the piano.)

   ____

7. *Luis se pone un suéter.* (Luis puts on a sweater.)

   ____

Answers:

2. _(Tú) vas a leer el documento._ (You're going to read the document.)
3. _(Él) va a bailar hoy._ (He's going to dance today.)
4. _(Nosotros) vamos a visitar a nuestros primos._
   (We're going to visit our cousins.)
5. _(Yo) voy a beber el café._ (I'm going to drink coffee.)
6. _Carla va a tocar el piano._ (Carla's going to play the piano.)
7. _Luis se va a poner un suéter._ (Luis is going to put on a sweater.)

The present progressive tense is used when an action is happening at the time of speaking.

The present progressive tense uses the gerund form of a verb, which replaces verb endings *-er* and *-ir* with *-iendo,* and verb ending *-ar* with *-ando.*

This is how you form the present progressive tense:

Subject + *estar* (conjugated) + gerund (verb ending in *-iendo* or *-ando*)

Listen to Track 157

Practice: Fill in the blanks with the appropriate conjugated form of *estar*, and the gerund. The first one has been done for you.

1. *Luisa está estudiando la lección.*
2. *Manuel y Rodrigo _____________ _____________ (abrir) las ventanas de la casa.*
3. *Nosotros _____________ _____________ (viajar) a Madrid.*
4. *Carla _____________ _____________ (comer) una ensalada.*
5. *Yo _____________ _____________ (limpiar) la cocina.*

Answer key:

2. *Manuel y Rodrigo están abriendo las ventanas de la casa.*
3. *Nosotros estamos viajando a Madrid.*
4. *Carla está comiendo una ensalada.*
5. *Yo estoy limpiando la cocina.*

Listen to Track 158

Practice: Translate from English to Spanish.

1. Lili is cooking. (*cocinar*)

   ____

2. The boys are playing soccer. (*jugar al fútbol*)

   ____

3. Grandma is dancing in the kitchen. (*bailar en la cocina*)

   ____

4. We are studying English in class. (*estudiar inglés en clase*)

____

Answer key:

1. *Lili está cocinando.*
2. *Los niños están jugando al fútbol.*
3. *La abuela está bailando en la cocina.*
4. *Nosotras/nosotros estamos estudiando inglés en clase.*

Questions in Spanish have an inverted question mark at the front, and a normal question mark at the end. Yes/no questions in Spanish are very easy!

In writing, you only have to frame the statement with question marks to make it into a question. When asking yes/no questions in Spanish, like in English, raise your intonation (pitch and tone of voice) at the end of the question.

Listen to Track 159

Example: *Sabrina juega al tenis.* → *¿Sabrina juega al tenis?*
(Sabrina plays tennis. → Does Sabrina play tennis?)

Listen to Track 160

Practice: Turn these sentences into yes/no questions. The first one has been done for you.

1. *Manuel camina en el parque.* → *¿Manuel camina en el parque?*
   (Manuel walks in the park. → Does Manuel walk in the park?)

2. *Tienes mucho dinero.* → ______________________________
   (You have a lot of money.)

3. *Hacen su tarea.* → ______________________________
   (They do their homework.)

4. *Ustedes leen libros.* → ______________________________
   (You read books.)

Answers:
1. *¿Manuel camina en el parque?*
2. *¿Tienes mucho dinero?*
3. *¿Hacen su tarea?*
4. *¿Ustedes leen libros?*

Practice: Find Spanish sentences throughout the workbook that can be turned into yes/no questions. Practice both writing and saying yes/no questions in Spanish!

¿Qué? – What?

The question word *¿qué?* is used to ask for general information in Spanish. It can be followed by many different verbs.

Here are some common *¿qué?* questions:

Listen to Track 161

¿Qué es?	(What is?)
¿Qué haces?	(What do you do?)
¿Qué te gusta?	(What do you like?)
¿Qué estudias?	(What do you study?)

Listen to Track 162

Practice: Translate the Spanish to English.

¿Qué le gusta hacer?	What do you like to do?
¿Qué se pone? (usted)	
¿Qué tienes?	
¿Qué practican?	
¿Qué les gusta jugar a los hermanos?	
¿Qué tiene que hacer? (usted)	
¿Qué escuchamos?	
¿Qué tienen?	
¿Qué escribe? (ella)	

Answers:

¿Qué se pone? (usted)	What do you wear?
¿Qué tienes?	What do you have?
¿Qué practican?	What do they practice?
¿Qué les gusta jugar a los hermanos?	What do the brothers like to play?
¿Qué tiene que hacer? (usted)	What do you have to do?
¿Qué escuchamos?	What do we listen to?
¿Qué tienen?	What do they have?
¿Qué escribe? (ella)	What does she write?

Listen to Track 163

Practice: In pairs, make *¿qué?* questions using the following verbs, then try answering each other's questions. To make original questions, try thinking of complements, like the ones underlined below:

ver (to see/watch)	*¿Qué ves el fin de semana?* (What do you watch on the weekend?) *¿Qué ves en la televisión?* (What do you watch on TV?)
comer (to eat)	
beber (to drink)	
leer (to read)	

¿Qué Hora Es? – What Time is It?

To ask about the time in Spanish, use the expression *¿Qué hora es?*

Answer with **"son las"** number **"y"** minutes, except for one o'clock.

Listen to Track 164

¿Qué hora es?	(What time is it?)
1:00 am/pm. Es la una.	(1:00 am or pm. It's one o'clock.)
9:20 am. Son las nueve y veinte de la mañana.	(9:20 am. It's twenty past nine in the morning.)
3:30 pm. Son las tres y treinta de la tarde.	(3:30 pm. It's three thirty in the afternoon.)

Here are other common Spanish expressions to tell the time:

Listen to Track 165

en punto (on the dot, "sharp")

Example: 5:00 *Son las cinco en punto.*
(It's five o'clock.)

y cuarto (quarter, or 15 minutes)

Example: 8:15 *Son las ocho y cuarto.* (It's quarter past eight.)

y media (half past, or 30 minutes)

Example: 10:30 *Son las diez y media.* (It's half past ten.)

menos cuarto (15 minutes until, or 45 minutes)

Example: 3:45 *Son las tres menos cuarto.* (It's quarter 'til four.)

de la madrugada (in the [very early] morning)

Example: 3:00am *Son las tres en punto de la madrugada.*
(It's seven o'clock in the early morning.)

de la mañana (in the morning)

Example: 7:00am *Son las siete en punto de la mañana.*
(It's seven o'clock in the morning.)

de la tarde (in the afternoon)

Example: 3:00pm   *Son las tres en punto de la tarde.*
(It's seven o'clock in the afternoon.)

de la noche (in the evening/at night)

Example: 7:00pm   *Son las siete en punto de la noche.*
(It's seven o'clock in the evening.)

Practice: Write the time in Spanish. Use the time expressions when applicable.

1. 7:45 ____
2. 1:00 ____
3. 12:15 ____
4. 3:00am ____
5. 8:55 ____
6. 1:30pm ____
7. 6:07am ____
8. 5:42 ____
9. 2:22 ____
10. 11:09 ____
11. 4:17 ____

Listen to Track 166

Answer:

1. 7:45   *Son las siete menos cuarto.*
2. 1:00   *Es la una.*
3. 12:15   *Son las doce y cuarto.*
4. 3:00am   *Son las tres en punto de la madrugada.*
5. 8:55   *Son las ocho y cincuenta y cinco./Son las nueve menos cinco.*
6. 1:30pm   *Es la una y media de la tarde.*
7. 6:07am   *Son las seis y siete de la mañana.*
8. 5:42   *Son las cinco y cuarenta y dos./Son las seis menos dieciocho.*
9. 2:22   *Son las dos y veintidós.*
10. 11:09pm   *Son las once y nueve de la noche.*
11. 4:17   *Son las cuatro y diecisiete.*

¿A Qué Hora? – At What Time is It?

The question "*¿a qué hora es?*" is generally used to find out the exact time an event takes place. Let's see how to ask.

Listen to Track 167

¿A qué hora es la película?	(What time is the movie?)
La película es a las 7:00 pm.	(The movie is at 7:00 pm.)
¿A qué hora es tu clase de español?	(What time is your Spanish class?)
Mi clase de español es a las 5:00 pm.	(My Spanish class is at 5:00pm.)

We can use the following structure to ask about daily routines.

¿A qué hora + verb (conjugated) + complement?

Practice: In pairs, ask about your daily routines.

Listen to Track 168

For example: *¿A qué hora vas a la escuela?* (What time do you go to school?)
    A las 7:00 am. (At 7:00 am.)

Listen to Track 169

Practice: Write your own questions and answers similar to the examples above. Use the scenarios below to base your questions on.

ir a casa (go home)

ir al parque (go to the park)

hacer la tarea (do the homework)

Sample answers: *¿A qué hora vas a su casa?*
    ¿A qué hora vas al parque?
    ¿A qué hora haces tu tarea?

¿Quién? – Who?

When we ask about a person in Spanish, it is necessary to use the word *¿quién?* in the singular. When we're asking about multiple persons or people, we use *¿quiénes?*

Listen to Track 170

Example: *¿Quién es?*   (Who is it*?)*

                   ¿Quiénes son?   (Who are they?)

Practice: In pairs, show pictures of people you both know (friends or celebrities), and ask who they are in Spanish.

Example: *¿Quién es?*   (Who is it?)

                   Ella es Jennifer Aniston.   (She is Jennifer Aniston.)

                   Él es nuestro maestro.   (He is our teacher.)

After that, ask each other *¿Quién eres?* (Who are you?) Talk about yourselves in terms of relationships or characteristics. See the chapters about the verb *ser* (to be) and adjectives if you're struggling to find ways to describe yourself.

Example: ¿Quién eres?

                   Soy estudiante. Yo tengo 15 años y me gusta jugar videojuegos.
                   (I am a student. I'm 15 years old and I like to play video games.)

¿Dónde? – Where?

To ask about a place in Spanish, the expression *¿dónde?* is used, followed by the verbs *estar*, and *quedar (estar ubicado)*, among others.

Examples:

Listen to Track 171

¿Dónde está el aeropuerto?	(Where is the airport?)
¿Dónde queda tu casa?	(Where is your house?)
¿Dónde está mi libro?	(Where is my book?)
¿Dónde queda la escuela?	(Where is the school?)

Practice: In pairs, ask each other where a family member, friend, or classmate is right now. Then imagine you are at the mall, the supermarket, or at home. Ask each other where you and your friend, or other people and objects, might be in those places. Ask questions with *¿dónde?*

Listen to Track 172

Sample answers:

¿Dónde estás?	Where are you?
Yo estoy en mi casa.	I am at home.
¿Dónde está Mari?	Where is Mari?
Está en la zona de frutas.	She is in the fruit section.
¿Dónde están tus amigos?	Where are your friends?
Mis amigos están en el supermercado.	They are in the supermarket.

¿Cuándo? – When?

¿*Cuándo* + verb + subject (optional) + complement(s)?

Listen to Track 173

The expression used to ask about a time in Spanish is *¿cuándo?* or "when?" It is followed by a verb that agrees with the following subject, whether explicitly voiced or not. Let's see some examples below.

¿Cuándo es...?	(When is...?)
¿Cuándo vienes?	(When are you coming?)
¿Cuándo vas?	(When are you going?)

Notice that *vienes* and *vas* are conjugated according to the subject *"tu,"* which is implied and not explicitly stated in the question.

Examples: *¿Cuándo es tu cumpleaños?* (When is your birthday?)
¿Cuándo vienes a la escuela? (When are you coming to school?)
¿Cuándo vas a la universidad? (When do you go to college?)

Listen to Track 174

Practice: Make questions using *¿cuándo?* for the expressions below.

1. *Es el cumpleaños de tu mamá.* (It's your mom's birthday.)

   ____

2. *tu + venir a mi casa.* (you cou come to my house)

   ____

3. *nosotros + estudiar* (we study)

   ____

4. *tu + ir a la fiesta.* (you go to the party)

   ____

5. *ellos/ellas + llegar* (they arrive)

   ____

Answers:

1. *¿Cuándo es el cumpleaños de tu mamá?*
2. *¿Cuándo vienes a mi casa?*
3. *¿Cuándo estudiamos?*
4. *¿Cuándo vas a la fiesta?*
5. *¿Cuándo llegan?*

¿Cuál? – Which One?

The expressions *¿cuál?* or *¿cuáles?* are used when asking someone to choose from multiple options. They can be things, animals, people, or situations.

Listen to Track 175

(Pictures of two objects) *¿Cuál es tu preferido?* (Which one do you prefer?)

(Picture of several objects) *¿Cuáles te gustan?* (Which ones do you like?)

Note: *¿Cuál?* (singular) is used to select **one option only**.
¿Cuáles? (plural) means one can choose **multiple options**.

Here are other *¿Cuál/Cuáles?* questions:

¿Cuál es tu favorito?	(Which is your favorite?)
¿Cuál es el tuyo?	(Which one is yours?)

Listen to Track 176

Practice: *Preguntas de opción múltiple* (multiple choice questions)

Create your own fun multiple choice questions, and in pairs, make each other's questions. Make sure to use *¿Cuál/Cuáles?* to show if your partner can only choose one option or multiple options.

| 1: *¿Cuáles son las clases más fáciles en la escuela?* (Which are the easiest classes in school?)

 a: *la hora de estudio libre* (study hall)
 b: *la clase de arte* (art class)
 c: *las matemáticas* (math)
 d: *la educación física* (physical education)
 e: *otro* (other):

 __________________________ | 2: *¿Cuál es tu comida favorita?* (Which is your favorite food?)

 a: *la pizza*
 b: *el helado* (ice cream)
 c: *la bola de masa hervida* (dumplings)
 d: *las papas fritas* (potato chips)
 e: *otro* (other):

 __________________________ |
| 3: *¿Cuál*

 a: <br> b: <br> c: <br> d: | 4: *¿Cuáles*

 a: <br> b: <br> c: <br> d: |

¿Cuántos/As? – How Many?

¿Cuántos(as)? is used to ask how many there are of something. The question word is followed by the noun you want to know the quantity of.

Make sure to follow the gender and number of the noun following the question word!

For example:

Listen to Track 177

¿Cuántas computadoras hay en el escritorio?	How many computers are on the desk?
¿Cuántos libros tienes?	How many books do you have?

"Computadoras" are feminine and plural, so we use ***¿cuántas?*** *"Libros"* are masculine and plural, so we use ***¿cuántos?***

Listen to Track 178

Practice: Fill in the blanks with the appropriate agreement for ***¿cuántos(as)?***

¿_________ horas toma viajar desde aquí a Australia?	How many hours does it take to travel from here to Australia?
¿_________ leche tomas al día?	How much milk do you drink per day?
¿_________ mantequilla pones a tu desayuno?	How much butter do you put on your breakfast?
¿_________ cuesta este juguete?	How much is this toy?
¿_________ cuestan esos?	How much are those?

Answer key:

¿Cuántas horas toma viajar desde aquí a Australia?	How many hours does it take to travel from here to Australia?
¿Cuánta leche tomas al día?	How much milk do you drink per day?
¿Cuánta mantequilla pones a tu desayuno?	How much butter do you put on your breakfast?
¿Cuánto cuesta este juguete?	How much is this toy?
¿Cuánto cuestan esos?	How much are those?

¿Cómo? Y ¿Por Qué? – How? and Why?

The question **¿cómo?** (how?) is used if you want to know the way to do something, the state of health of a person, and how someone is named.

For example:

Listen to Track 179

¿Cómo estás?	(How are you?)
¿Cómo está tu familia?	(How is your family?)
¿Cómo se prepara el arroz?	(How is rice prepared?)
¿Cómo vas a la universidad?	(How do you go to the university?)
¿Cómo te llamas?	(What is your name?)

Practice: With a partner, ask each other your own *¿cómo?* questions similar to the examples given above.

The question **¿por qué?** (why?) is used to know the reasons or motives for something. Let's see how it is used.

Listen to Track 180

¿Por qué te gusta estudiar?	(Why do you like to study?)
Porque es muy bueno.	(Because it is very good.)
Hoy voy a la Universidad.	(Today I am going to the university.)
¿Por qué?	(Why?)
Porque tengo un examen.	(Because I have an exam.)
Daniela está cocinando mucho.	(Daniela is cooking a lot.)
¿Por qué?	(Why?)
Porque hay una fiesta.	(Because there is a party.)

Practice: With a partner, ask each other your own *¿por qué?* questions similar to the examples given above.

Activity: Preguntas de Información – Information Questions

Based on the questions we've learned to ask in previous sections, try making some information questions of your own. In groups of three, try asking each other questions and practice answering information questions in Spanish.

Listen to Track 181

¿Dónde es?	Where is?
¿Qué hora es?	What time is it?
¿Quién?	Who?
¿Qué?	What?
¿A qué hora es?	At what time is it?
¿Cuánto cuesta?	How much is it?
¿Cuál?	Which?
¿Cuándo?	When?
¿Por qué?	Why?

For example: *¿Quién es la persona que está en esta foto?*
                        (Who is the person who is in this photo?)

The conversations can be about family, places, interests, and subjects. Use the space below to plan out your questions.

____

____

____

____

____

Una Entrevista – An Interview

Listen to Track 182

Are you ready for an interview? Let's answer some questions about you.
Practice: Answer the following questions in Spanish.

1. *¿Cómo te llamas?*
   ____

2. *¿Cuántos años tienes?*
   ____

3. *¿Dónde vives?*
   ____

4. *¿Cómo se llama tu papá?*
   ____

5. *¿Cuántos hermanos y hermanas tienes?*
   ____

6. *¿Cuándo es tu cumpleaños?*
   ____

7. *¿A qué hora te despiertas?*
   ____

8. *¿Cuál es tu serie de televisión favorita?*
   ____

9. *¿A qué le tienes miedo?*
   ____

10. *¿Qué prefieres, los perros o los gatos?*
    ____

11. *¿Sabes cocinar?*
    ____

Sample answers:

1. *Me llamo José Eduardo.*
2. *Tengo 17 años.*
3. *Vivo en México.*
4. *Se llama José.*
5. *Tengo un hermano y una hermana.*
6. *Mi cumpleaños es el siete de febrero.*
7. *Me despierto a las seis de la mañana.*
8. *La casa de papel.*
9. *A las arañas.*
10. *Prefiero los gatos.*
11. *Sí, yo sé cocinar.*

"Gustar" – To Like

The verb to express likes in Spanish is ***gustar***, though it literally means "it is pleasing to me." Use it before a noun to say you like something, or before an infinitive verb to say you like an activity.

Listen to Track 183

Subject	*gustar* (to like)
Yo	*me gusta(n)*
Tú	*te gusta(n)*
Él, ella, usted	*le gusta(n)*
Vos, vosotros, vosotras	*os gusta(n)*
Nosotros, nosotras	*nos gusta(n)*
Ellos, ellas, ustedes	*les gusta(n)*

Note: use *gusta* with singular nouns, and *gustan* for plural nouns.

Listen to Track 184

Practice: In your class, walk around and ask your peers, *¿Qué te gusta a ti?*

If you're formally asking your teacher, use *¿Qué le gusta a usted?*

If you're asking several classmates, use *¿Qué les gusta a ustedes?*

Make sure to write down what you learn about your classmates below!

Sample conversations:

¿Qué te gusta a ti?	What do you like?
Me gustan mucho mis perros.	I like my dogs very much.
¿Qué les gusta a ustedes?	What do you like? (plural)
Nos gusta la escalada en roca.	We like rock climbing.

No Me Gusta – I Don't Like

Practice: Look at the food below and state whether you like or dislike them. Use *me gusta(n)* or *no me gusta(n)*.

Listen to Track 185

Example: *Me gusta la sandía.* (I like watermelon.)
            Me gustan las fresas. (I like strawberries.)

El helado (ice cream)   1. ______________________________

Los pepinos (cucumbers)   2. ______________________________

Los plátanos (bananas)   3. ______________________________

Las manzanas (apples)   4. ______________________________

El queso (cheese)   5. ______________________________

La leche (milk)   6. ______________________________

El pollo (chicken)   7. ______________________________

El pan (bread)   8. ______________________________

El pescado (fish)   9. ______________________________

La carne de res (beef)   10. ______________________________

La carne de cerdo (pork)   11. ______________________________

Las naranjas (oranges)   12. ______________________________

El chocolate (chocolate)   13. ______________________________

La cebolla (onion)   14. ______________________________

El aguacate (avocado)   15. ______________________________

You can express preferences using *gustar* (to like) and the comparative adjective *más* (more). *Gusta(n) más* literally translates to "to like more."

Listen to Track 186

Practice: Answer the questions below with your own answers in Spanish.

Example: *¿Te gusta más el cupcake o el pastel?* (Do you prefer a cupcake or a cake?)
  Me gusta más el cupcake. (I prefer the cupcake.)

1. *¿Te gusta más el arroz, o la pasta?*
   (Do you prefer rice or pasta?)
2. *¿A ellas les gustan más los zapatos, o las sandalias?*
   (Do they prefer shoes or sandals?)
3. *¿A ustedes les gusta más estudiar español o estudiar italiano?*
   (Do you [plural] prefer studying Spanish or Italian?)
4. *¿A él le gusta más ir al parque de diversiones o ir a comer?*
   (Does he prefer going to the amusement park or to eat?)
5. *¿A usted le gusta más el café o el té?*
   (Do you [formal] prefer coffee or tea?)
6. *¿A ella le gustan más los brownies o las galletas?*
   (Does she prefer brownies or cookies?)

"Dar" – To Give

The verb **dar** (to give) is a very common, but irregular Spanish verb.

Subject	dar (to give)
Yo	doy
Tú	das
Él, ella, usted	da
Vos	das
Vosotros, vosotras	dáis
Nosotros, nosotras	damos
Ustedes	dan
Ellos, ellas	dan

This verb has many uses. Dar is also a pronominal verb (**darse**) and can be combined with the reflexive pronouns **me, te, le, nos, os,** and **les** to direct the action of giving.

Examples: *David **me da** muchos regalos.*
(David gives me many gifts.)

*Daniel **nos da** el desayuno.*
(Daniel gives us breakfast.)

Practice: Fill in the blanks with *dar* and the correct reflexive pronoun.

1. *Mari _____ _______ alimento a su perrito.* (Mari gives food to her puppy.)
2. *Nuestros padres _______ _________ helados.* (Our parents give us ice cream.)
3. *Quiero _________ ______ muchos regalos.* (I want to give you many gifts.)

Answer key:

1. *Mari le da alimento a su perrito.*
2. *Nuestros padres nos dan muchos helados.*
3. *Quiero darte muchos regalos.*

Otros Usos de "Dar" – Other Uses of "To Give"

"*Dar*" is used in other Spanish phrases and expressions, including:

When an object is faced toward something or takes you somewhere: *dar a*

Listen to Track 189

Example: *Mi ventana da a la playa.* (My window faces the beach.)
Esta puerta da a la cocina. (This door takes you to the kitchen.)

When feeding an animal or a person: *dar de comer a*

Example: *Ellos le dan de comer a su hámster.* (They feed their hamster.)

When someone or something is telling the hour: *dar la hora*

Example: ¿Me puedes dar la hora? (Could you tell me what time it is?)

When someone gives or holds a hand: *dar la mano*

Example: *Tu me das la mano.* (You give me your hand.)

To thank: *dar las gracias*

Example: *Damos las gracias por la comida.* (We give thanks for the food.)

When someone goes for a walk: *dar un paseo*

Example: *Ella da un paseo por el parque.* (She goes for a walk in the park.)

A. To say good morning/good night: *dar los buenos días/las buenas noches*

Example: *Yo doy los buenos días a mi vecino.*
(I say good morning to my neighbor.)

Practice: Write the sentences in Spanish.

1. The window faces the street. ________________________
2. I feed my cat. ________________________
3. She says good morning to her mom. ________________________
4. I give thanks for your help. ________________________

Listen to Track 190

Answers:

1. *La ventana da a la calle.*
2. *Yo le doy de comer a mi gato.*
3. *Ella dice buenos días a su mamá.*
4. *Doy gracias por tu ayuda.*

Listen to Track 191

Practice: Complete the sentence in Spanish.

1. *Ese reloj ya ____ _____ la hora, necesita pilas.*
   (That clock doesn't tell the time anymore. It needs batteries.)
2. *Le ____ __ ________ zanahorias a mi perro.*
   (I feed carrots to my dog.)
3. *Yo siempre ____ ____ ________ _____ en la escuela.*
   (I always say good morning at school.)
4. *Cuando alguien te ayuda tienes que ____ ____ ______.*
   (When somebody helps you, you have to say thanks.)
5. *Estoy aburrido, vamos a ____ __ _____ por el bosque.*
   (I am bored. Let's go for a walk in the forest.)
6. *Mi papá __ ____ _____ _____ con un beso.*
   (My father says good morning with a kiss.)
7. *El refrigerador __ __ la televisión.*
   (The fridge faces the TV.)
8. *No debes ____ __ _____ después de estornudar en ella.*
   (You must not give your hand after sneezing on it.)
9. *Nosotros no le ______ __ ______ a los animales del zoológico.*
   (We don't feed the zoo animals.)

Answers:

1. *Este reloj ya <u>no da</u> la hora, necesita pilas.*
2. *Le <u>doy de comer</u> zanahorias a mi perro.*
3. *Yo siempre <u>doy los buenos días</u> en la escuela.*
4. *Cuando alguien te ayuda tienes que <u>dar las gracias</u>.*
5. *Estoy aburrido, vamos a <u>dar un paseo</u> por el bosque.*
6. *Mi papá <u>da los buenos días</u> con un beso.*
7. *El refrigerador <u>da a</u> la televisión.*
8. *No debes <u>dar la mano</u> después de estornudar en ella.*
9. *Nosotros no le <u>damos de comer</u> a los animales del zoológico.*

"Saber" Vs. "Conocer" – To Know

Saber (to know) is used in Spanish to express knowledge of information or facts. *Saber* is also used to express an ability. *Saber* is an irregular verb. The conjugation is as follows:

Listen to Track 192

Subject	*saber* (to know)
Yo	*sé*
Tú	*sabes*
Él, ella, usted	*sabe*
Vos	*sabés*
Vosotros, vosotras	*sabéis*
Nosotros, nosotras	*sabemos*
Ustedes	*saben*
Ellos, ellas	*saben*

In the sentence below, the **subject knows about a fact**.

Listen to Track 193

Yo sé que Susana no come ensaladas.
(I know Susana does not eat salads.)

In this sentence, the **subject has an ability**.

Daniel sabe cocinar. (Daniel knows how to cook.)

Conocer (to know) is used to express familiarity. In other words, a person knows this place, person, or concept because they've seen or heard of it before. As an irregular verb, be sure to memorize its conjugated forms!

Listen to Track 194

Subject	*conocer* (to know)
Yo	conozco
Tú	conoces
Él, ella, usted	conoce
Vos	conocés
Vosotros, vosotras	conocéis
Nosotros, nosotras	conocemos
Ustedes	conocen
Ellos, ellas	conocen

Listen to Track 195

Practice: Complete the sentences with the verb *saber* or *conocer*.

Mi papá _________ *manejar el auto.*	(My father knows how to drive the car.)
Mi familia _________ *la zona.*	(My family knows the area.)
Nosotros ___________ *nadar.*	(We know how to swim.)
Las niñas _________ *jugar con la pelota.*	(The girls know how to play with the ball.)
Mis hijos _________ *mucha Historia.*	(My kids know a lot of history.)
Tú _________ *a Mari.*	(You know Mari.)

Answer key:

Mi papá <u>sabe</u> manejar el auto.	(My father knows how to drive the car.)
Mi familia <u>conoce</u> la zona.	(My family knows the area.)
Nosotros <u>sabemos</u> nadar.	(We know how to swim.)
Las niñas <u>saben</u> jugar con la pelota.	(The girls know how to play with the ball.)
Mis hijos <u>saben</u> mucha Historia.	(My kids know a lot of history.)
Tú <u>conoces</u> a Mari.	(You know Mari.)

Poder – To be Able To

The word *poder* in Spanish means the same as "be able to" or "can" when it is used in front of another verb.

Listen to Track 196

Subject	*poder* (to be able to / can)
Yo	*puedo*
Tú	*puedes*
Vos	*podés*
Él, ella, usted	*puede*
Nosotros, nosotras	*podemos*
Vosotros, vosotras	*podéis*
Ustedes	*pueden*
Ellos, ellas	*pueden*

The verb that follows the word *poder* is used in the infinitive form. For example:

Listen to Track 197

> *Yo puedo nadar.* (I can swim.)
> *Tú puedes escribir.* (You can write.)
> *¿Puedes saltar la cuerda?* (Can you jump rope?)
> *Sí, yo puedo saltar la cuerda.* (Yes, I can jump rope.)
> *No, yo no puedo saltar la cuerda.* (No, I can't jump rope.)

Practice: Write the sentences in Spanish.

She can play the piano.	
You can run.	*Tú*
We can eat pizza.	*Nosotras*
They can write.	*Ellos*
I can read.	
He can learn.	
You can talk.	*Vos*

Listen to Track 198

Answers:

She can play the piano.	*Ella puede tocar el piano.*
You can run.	*Tú puedes correr.*
We can eat pizza.	*Nosotras podemos comer pizza.*
They can write.	*Ellos pueden escribir.*
I can read.	*Yo puedo leer.*
He can learn.	*Él puede aprender.*
You can talk.	*Vos podés hablar.*

Listen to Track 199

Practice: Answer the questions with complete sentences.

Example: *¿Puedes leer?* <u>*Sí, yo puedo leer.*</u>
<u>*No, yo no puedo leer.*</u>

1. *¿Puedes ver?* _______________________
2. *¿Puedes pintar?* _______________________
3. *¿Puedes escribir?* _______________________
4. *¿Puedes trabajar?* _______________________
5. *¿Puedes escuchar?* _______________________

Answers:

1. <u>*Sí, yo puedo ver. No, yo no puedo ver.*</u>
2. <u>*Sí, yo puedo pintar. No, yo no puedo pintar.*</u>
3. <u>*Sí, yo puedo escribir. No, yo no puedo escribir.*</u>
4. <u>*Sí, yo puedo trabajar. No, yo no puedo trabajar.*</u>
5. <u>*Sí, yo puedo escuchar. No, yo no puedo escuchar.*</u>

Listen to Track 200

Practice: Write the appropriate question.

Example: *Sí, él puede jugar.* <u>*¿Él puede jugar?*</u>

1. *No, ella no puede reír.* _______________________
2. *Sí, ellos pueden venir.* _______________________
3. *Sí, yo puedo cantar.* _______________________
4. *No, vosotros no podéis gritar.* _______________________
5. *Sí, tú puedes comer.* _______________________

Answers:

1. *¿(Ella) puede reír?*
2. *¿(Ellos) pueden venir?*
3. *¿(Tú) puedes cantar?*
4. *¿(Nosotros) podemos gritar?*
5. *¿(Yo) puedo comer?*

Listen to Track 201

Practice: Complete the sentences.

Example: *Yo <u>puedo tomar</u> refresco.*
      (can drink)

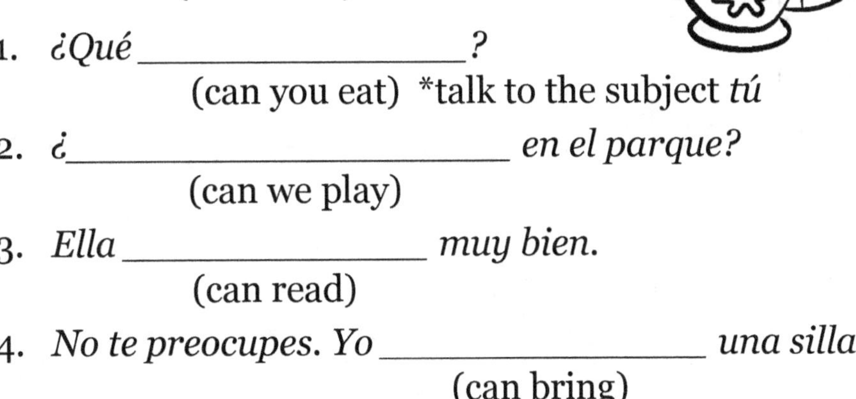

1. *¿Qué______________?*
    (can you eat) *talk to the subject *tú*

2. *¿_________________ en el parque?*
    (can we play)

3. *Ella______________ muy bien.*
    (can read)

4. *No te preocupes. Yo______________ una silla.*
    (can bring)

Answers:

1. *¿Qué puedes comer?*
2. *¿Podemos jugar en el parque?*
3. *Ella puede leer muy bien.*
4. *No te preocupes. Yo puedo traer una silla.*

El Infinitivo – The Infinitive

In Spanish, the infinitive is the form of the verbs when they finish with "*-ar*", "*-er*", or "*-ir*". It is used after some prepositions.

Listen to Track 202

Example: *al leer.* (upon reading)
   sin preguntar. (without asking)

Some prepositions used before infinitive verbs are:

Spanish	English
sin	without
al	upon
antes de	before
después de	after

Practice: Write the following statements in Spanish.

1. after eating   ______________________
2. before jumping   ______________________
3. upon waking up   ______________________
4. without talking   ______________________
5. after learning   ______________________
6. upon speaking   ______________________

Listen to Track 203

Answers:

1. after eating   *después de comer*
2. before jumping   *antes de saltar*
3. upon waking up   *al despertar*
4. without talking   *sin hablar*
5. after learning   *después de aprender*
6. upon speaking   *al hablar*

Practice: Write the sentences in Spanish.

1. They walk without talking.   *Ellos* ______________________
2. You get out upon finishing your exam.   ______________________
3. You run before going to sleep.   *Vos* ______________________
4. I read without stopping.   ______________________

Listen to Track 204

Answers:

1. *Ellos caminan sin hablar.*
2. *Tú sales al terminar tu examen.*
3. *Vos corréis antes de ir a dormir.*
4. *Yo leo sin parar.*

The infinitive is not only used after certain prepositions. We also use the infinitive after some verbs and verb phrases. These include:

Listen to Track 205

Verb/verb phrase	Example
tener que	*Tengo que salir.* (I have to go out.)
hay que	*Hay que comprar leche.* (We have to buy milk.)
saber	*¿Sabes escribir?* (Do you know how to write?)
gustar	*Me gusta bailar.* (I like to dance.)
ir a	*Vamos a trabajar.* (We are going to work.)

Listen to Track 206

Practice: Complete the sentences in Spanish.

1. *A ella le______________________ ____________________.*
   (She likes to travel.)

2. *Nosotros________________ ____________ ________________ temprano.*
   (We have to go out early.) *use the verb *tener que*.

3. *Yo no_______ _________ muy bien.*
   (I don't know how to cook very well.)

4. *__________ __________ ____________________ a mis abuelos.*
   (We have to visit my grandparents.) *use the verb *hay que*.

Answers:

1. *A ella le gusta viajar.*
2. *Nosotros tenemos que salir temprano.*
3. *Yo no sé cocinar muy bien.*
4. *Hay que visitar a mis abuelos.*

El Imperativo – The Imperative

The imperative is used in Spanish to give orders and advice. To form the imperative, take the first-person present conjugation of a verb. Get rid of the -o ending and replace it with the endings below:

Listen to Track 207

Subject	-ar (caminar)	-er (leer)	-ir (abrir)
Tú	camin**a**	le**e**	ab**re**
Usted	camin**e**	le**a**	ab**ra**
Nosotros, nosotras	camin**emos**	le**amos**	abr**amos**
Vosotros, vosotras	camin**ad**	le**ed**	abr**id**
Ustedes	camin**en**	le**an**	ab**ran**

Listen to Track 208

Practice: Fill in the blanks with the correct imperative conjugated verb. The first two problems have been answered for you. Note: the subject pronouns aren't used in the imperative, but we know who we're talking to based on the conjugated verb.

Example: *¡Estudia la lección!*
   Ve a clases todos los días. (Go to class every day.)

1. ¡_____________(tú - abrir) la ventana pronto! (Open the window quickly!)
2. _____________ (usted - escuchar) con atención. (Listen carefully.)
3. ¡No _____________(ustedes - correr) en la escuela! (Don't run at school!)
4. _____________ (vosotros/as - leer) el libro, por favor. (Read the book, please.)
5. ¡_____________ (nosotros/as - vivir) en Hawái! (Let's live in Hawaii!)
6. ¡No _____________ (tú - comer) mucho! (Don't eat too much!)

Answers:

1. *¡Abre la ventana pronto!*
2. *Escuche con atención.*
3. *¡No corran en la escuela!*
4. *Leed el libro, por favor.*
5. *¡Vivamos en Hawái!*
6. *¡No comas mucho!*

El Internet – The Internet

The Internet is relatively new, so many Spanish words related to the Internet are taken directly from English. Let's see the vocabulary.

Listen to Track 209

El Internet (the Internet)
wifi (Wi-Fi)
blog (blog)
página web (web page)
sitio web (website)
computadora (computer)
punto com (dot com)
descargar (to download)
cargar (to upload)
archivos adjuntos (attached files)
archivo (file)
enlace/link (link)
negrita (bold)

página principal (home page)
contraseña (password)
correo (email)
suscribirse (subscribe)
bandeja de entrada (inbox)
mensaje directo (DM - direct message)
memoria (memory)
memoria USB (USB memory stick)
dar click (to click)
canal de youtube (YouTube channel)
tik tok (TikTok)
perfil (profile)

Listen to Track 210

Practice: Complete the sentences with the correct words.

1. *Lee bien las palabras que están en* ______________. (Read the words in **bold** carefully)
2. *No puedo entrar. Olvidé mi* ______________________. (I can't log in. I forgot my **password**.)
3. *Tengo que* ______________ *muchos archivos.* (I have a lot of files to **download**.)
4. *Regresa a la* ______________ ____________. (Go back to the **home page**.)
5. *Este* ____________ *es muy grande. No cabe en la memoria.* (This **file** is too big. It won't fit in the memory.)

6. *Juan escribe un* _____________ *para su mamá.* (Juan writes an **email** to his mother.)
7. *Da click en ese* _____________ *para ver el video.* (Click on that **link** to see the video.)

Answers:

1. *Lee bien las palabras que están en negrita.*
2. *No puedo entrar. Olvidé mi contraseña.*
3. *Tengo que descargar muchos archivos.*
4. *Regresa a la página principal.*
5. *Este archivo es muy grande. No cabe en la memoria.*
6. *Juan escribe un correo para su mamá.*
7. *Da click en ese link para ver el video.*

Repaso – Review

Practice: Write the sentences in Spanish.

1. My shoes are brown. _______________________
2. Do you want to go shopping? _______________________
3. This is my favorite blouse. _______________________
4. It is cold outside. Wear a sweater! _______________________
5. How much money do you have? _______________________
6. Where is my jacket? _______________________
7. I need a new t-shirt. _______________________

Listen to Track 211

Answers:

1. *Mis zapatos son cafés.*
2. *¿Quieres ir de compras?*
3. *Esta es mi blusa favorita.*
4. *Hace frío afuera. ¡Usa un suéter!*
5. *¿Cuánto dinero tienes?*
6. *¿Dónde está mi chamarra?*
7. *Yo necesito una nueva playera.*

Listen to Track 212

Practice: Write the sentences in English.

1. *¿Dónde está mi corbata?* _______________________
2. *María lleva puesta una falda amarilla.* _______________________
3. *Me gusta este traje de baño.* _______________________
4. *Estos calcetines son muy caros.* _______________________
5. *Ese vestido cuesta 300 pesos.* _______________________
6. *¿Cuántos pantalones tienes?* _______________________

Answers:

1. Where is my tie?
2. Maria is wearing a yellow dress.
3. I like this bathing suit.
4. These socks are very expensive.
5. This dress costs 300 pesos.
6. How many pairs of pants do you have?

Conclusion

Congratulations on finishing this book. We at My Daily Spanish are proud of you and hope you continue learning Spanish, just a little every day, from listening to Spanish music to watching telenovelas – it doesn't have to be boring and difficult to learn Spanish!

If you liked the Spanish Teen Workbook, we have other books available at My Daily Spanish store and Amazon. Feel free to browse the different titles and leave us an honest review!

If you have any comments, questions, or suggestions about this book, we're always open to your feedback! Reach out to us at support@mydailyspanish.com. We'd be happy to hear from you.

You can also follow My Daily Spanish on social media. We regularly post educational and entertaining content related to Spanish culture and the language to keep you motivated and learning Spanish everyday.

- Facebook: facebook.com/mydailyspanish
- Instagram: @holamydailyspanish
- Twitter: @mydailyspanish
- Pinterest: pinterest.com/mydailyspanish

Keep in touch! And don't forget to practice your Spanish!

Remember: A little every day goes a long way.

¡Hasta luego!

My Daily Spanish Team

Audio Download Instructions

Copy and paste this link into your browser:

https://mydailyspanish.com/spanish-teen-workbook

You will be guided to a webpage on our site. There will be a button that reads:

Click here to download the audio

This link will take you to a Google Drive folder. Right click on the folder, and click "Download." The folder with the audio files should begin downloading.

There is also a backup link on the webpage that directly downloads the folder. The files you have downloaded will be saved in a .zip folder.

Note: This is a large file. Do not open it until your browser tells you that it has completed the download successfully (usually a few minutes on a broadband connection, but if your connection is unreliable it could take 10 to 20 minutes).

The files will be in your "Downloads" folder unless you have changed your settings. Extract them from the .zip folder and save them to your computer or copy to your preferred devices, *et voilà !* You can now listen to the audio anytime, anywhere.

In case you have questions, don't hesitate to contact us at:

support@mydailyspanish.com

MyDailySpanish.com is a website created to help busy learners learn Spanish. It is designed to provide a fun and fresh take on learning Spanish through:

- Helping you create a daily learning habit that you will stick to until you reach fluency, and
- Making learning Spanish as enjoyable as possible for people of all ages.

With the help of awesome content and tried-and-tested language learning methods, My Daily Spanish aims to be the best place on the web to learn Spanish.

The website is continuously updated with free resources and useful materials to help you learn Spanish. This includes grammar and vocabulary lessons plus culture topics to help you thrive in a Spanish-speaking location – perfect not only for those who wish to learn Spanish, but also for travellers planning to visit Spanish-speaking destinations.

For any questions, please email support@mydailyspanish.com.